MICHIG

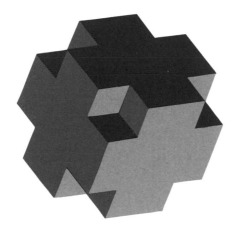

D1144520

This material comes to you through
your subscription to the
EDUCATIONAL RESEARCH SERVICE
American Association of School
Administrators and Research Division, NEA

LIBRARY
Michigan State
University

The School Administrator & Negotiation

Published by
AMERICAN ASSOCIATION OF SCHOOL ADMINISTRATORS
1201 SIXTEENTH STREET, N.W.
WASHINGTON, D.C. 20036

UNDERGRADUATE
LIBRARY

LB
2835
.A53
C. 2

Copyright 1968
American Association of School Administrators

All rights reserved.

No part of this document may be reproduced in any form without permission in writing from the publishers.

Stock number: 021-00482

66029
2-22-71

Table of Contents

Foreword

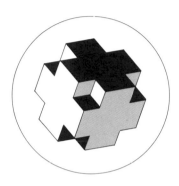

Were school administrators to name their most pressing current problems, negotiation would undoubtedly be near the top of the list, because it is persistently vexing to an increasing number of school administrators. Negotiation is accounting for marked changes in the working relationships of board members, superintendents, central office administrators and supervisors, principals, teachers, and other school personnel.

Professional teacher organizations are on the march. Many have repudiated acquiescence, abandoned passivity, and challenged the leadership of school administrators. Pressure for a more vital and greater share in educational decision making is evident in more and more school systems.

This teacher militancy has produced varied administrative reaction—dismay, disappointment, apprehension, and often antagonism. In some instances, however, the response has been one of acceptance. Those who have taken this attitude have done so in the belief that negotiation is not necessarily a destructive process, and there is a distinct possibility that it may be shaped so that it may actually strengthen teacher-administrator-board member relationships.

As AASA indicated in its publication on negotiation in the fall of 1966, the "days that were" in school relationships are fast fading, giving way to formalized guarantees of staff participation in policy making, the planning of formal give-and-take negotiation, and provisions for appeal in cases of impasse.

This new form of staff-administration-board interaction has become firmly rooted as a "way of life" in the public school enterprise. This is not to say, however, that these accords have been achieved without some tension, misunderstanding—even rancor—or without the expenditure of long hours of diligent dialogue and exhausting effort. Nevertheless, that impediments have been surmounted and deadlocks broken is testimony that compromises can be achieved and consensus may be reached.

The complexity, newness, and ultimate uncertainties of the negotiation process—frustrating as they are now or may become—are not likely to deter the onward press of teachers to share in planning for decision making on a widening range of educational matters. The times point in this direction. Even though school systems vary widely in the degree to which formalized negotiation is either an active or a benign issue, the trend toward its spread is unmistakable. While negotiation is a relatively recent force in the administration of schools, the manner in which administrators accept and adjust to its challenges will largely determine whether it develops into a persistently disruptive influence or becomes a constructive element in the administrative process.

Developing a strategem for "winning—at any cost—at the negotiation table"—even were this possible—is not a productive endeavor. Neither is suggesting recipes or prescriptions for negotiation. At best, only general guidelines can be offered.

State associations of school administrators, within the limitations of their own resources, hopefully can develop procedures, handbooks, and syllabi that provide specific assistance in helping administrators in local school systems become more proficient as negotiators.

This volume is focused upon the techniques and procedures of negotiation. While it does not prescribe a specific pattern or design for negotiation, it does suggest alternatives, believing that variations in state laws governing negotiation and circumstances in individual communities will determine the particular structure and most appropriate negotiation model for a given situation.

It is true, however, that considerable similarity exists in the structures for negotiation now in use throughout the country. It is profitable, therefore, to study the procedures being used and to take advantage of the experiences of others in formulating sound structures for negotiation.

To test the usefulness of this publication, a preliminary draft was prepared and field tested. This document, *The School Administrator and Negotiation,* is the result. The Executive Committee of the American Association of School Administrators hopes and believes that this publication will provide the basis for intelligent discussion and improved school administration.

GEORGE B. REDFERN
Associate Secretary
American Association of
School Administrators

FORREST E. CONNER
Executive Secretary
American Association of
School Administrators

Perspective

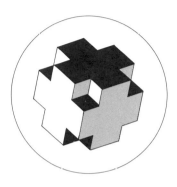

In an organization as diverse as the American Association of School Administrators it is difficult—if not impossible—to reach consensus on the form or direction negotiation should take. In states having negotiation statutes, the format of the process often is largely determined by law. In these instances, the options for freedom of action are obviously reduced. In the states not having laws, however, that mandate specific negotiation procedures, many options are open to teachers, administrators, and boards of education.

There is little if any disagreement about the importance of each school system providing the highest quality of educational service that its resources will afford, including teaching performance, physical facilities, equipment, supplies, supportive services, and leadership effort. These components, properly procured and deployed, give form and substance to the educational program; and attaining a high-quality program requires the fullest cooperation and solidarity of teachers, leadership personnel, and board members.

The question is how best to create the working conditions, climate of confidence, and dedication to purpose that will achieve quality education. It is becoming increasingly clear that methods of decision making in formulating educational policies and procedures have an important effect upon the performance of teachers, administrators, and board members.

The school system that has thought its way through the decision-making process and has developed, through cooperative effort, carefully formulated and written procedures for making educational determinations has a marked advantage over those that have not.

The trend is toward negotiation as the means for making educational decisions in an expanding range of areas. School systems will do well, therefore, to develop written policies and procedures for conducting negotiation. This endeavor should be achieved through the cooperative effort of teachers, administrators, and board members. As the provisions of the negotiation process are being formulated, purposes, roles, operational procedures, and implementation should be clearly defined and not left to chance.

Wherever possible, voluntary understandings should be reached on the form and structure of negotiation. Where stubborn resistance, undue inaction, or delay thwarts this, voluntary action may become less possible and involuntary measures may be sought to mandate negotiation.

This being the setting in which substantial changes are occurring in teacher-administrator-board member relationships, it may be useful to examine some significant issues inherent in the negotiation process. Obviously, there are many issues that could be considered; however, only five are presented here.

Issue 1

Does the education model for negotiation have to parallel that used in business and industry?/The initial temptation is to say "no" emphatically. A negative answer is predicated upon the belief that there are too many differences between the educational enterprise and business and industry. Product output and productivity are two of the most obvious differences, and in business and industry they can be calculated in rather precise terms so labor can bargain hard for its share.

Productivity in education is less precise and difficult to define in terms that make it possible to allocate credit for its attainment to any particular component in the educational process. While the greatest percentage of the educational dollar spent goes to instructional services (the teaching component), this is due to the nature of the educational process and has little to do with productivity. Thus, to negotiate for a larger share of this factor in education is very different from bargaining for a greater share of product output in business and industry.

Business and industry are organized as private profit-making enterprises. They are able to bargain with labor organizations knowing that if they have to raise prices or increase the productivity of their company to grant wage increases, they can make this decision as private entrepreneurs.

This is not the case in education. Since it is a public, rather than private, enterprise, the school system gets its financial support from taxes. Whether fiscally independent or dependent, a board of education operates within definite constraints in its power to grant higher salaries, greater fringe benefits, and better working conditions—all of which have definite price tags. This is a substantial difference.

A third difference is that education cannot measure outputs in relation to inputs in the same manner as business and industry can. It is difficult to measure the significance of teaching service as an educational input and equally as hard, if not more so, to relate it to output. In fact, it is not easy to get consensus on what is meant by educational inputs and outputs or their relationships to negotiation.

On the other hand, some similarities between education and business and industry make it possible to adapt certain of their techniques and procedures to negotiation in education. In doing so, it does not follow that educational negotiation is thus placed in a collective bargaining straightjacket and doomed to become a mere carbon copy of labor-management collective bargaining.

It is believed, however, that great effort should be made to design a negotiation model for education that will serve its unique needs better than one that merely parallels a labor-management format. It would seem reasonable that "if the unity and independence of the teaching profession, built up so painstakingly over the years, are to be preserved, laws must be developed which recognize the uniqueness of the educational enterprise." [1] Although this viewpoint is more or less academic in those states where the labor-management framework is largely mandated by statute, where the option is still open—as it is in the majority of states— a model for education would seem preferable.

Having argued for an educational model, however, does not prevent learning from the experiences of those who have developed considerable expertness in the art of negotiation by using business and industry collective bargaining procedures. If some of these techniques can be usefully adapted and used in negotiation, there is no reason to fear doing so.

Issue 2

Can and should the accountability principle be applied to all of the negotiating parties?/Some school administrators have raised the question of accountability in negotiation. They reason that the right to negotiate carries with it certain obligations on the part of the participants. Each party should be accountable for his actions, so it is argued.

It seems clear that members of boards of education can be held accountable for their actions by the public, whom they represent whether elected or appointed to their positions. The superintendent of schools, in turn, is accountable to the board of education, and he must answer to it for his decisions in negotiation.

It is not so clear to whom the organizations, which represent teachers, are accountable. In theory they too have obligations to the public, but it is not so evident how the public can require this accountability. Teachers themselves, when asked about this, often say that they are held accountable by the teaching profession itself.

---

[1] American Association of School Administrators. *School Administrators View Professional Negotiation*. Washington, D.C.: the Association, 1966. p. 50.

The relationship of board-to-public and superintendent-to-board is a different kind of accountability relationship than that of teacher-to-profession. The teaching profession itself probably has not attained a sufficient level of cohesion and maturity to discipline its members in a manner that warrants the conclusion that it can wield accountability controls over teacher organizations comparable to those of the other two negotiating parties.

If the teacher organization component in negotiation holds that it is accountable to the profession itself, it seems clear that the profession must be more vigorous in exerting the kind and level of discipline upon its members that makes accountability more meaningful. Time will determine whether this can become a reality rather than the aspiration it now appears to be.

Issue 3

What role does the superintendent play in negotiation? Is he "in" or "out" as a chief negotiator?/These are two of the most frequently raised questions in meetings at which negotiation is being discussed. Superintendents, themselves, are divided on the issue. There is general consensus, however, that every effort should be made to keep a school system a cohesive working unit and as free as possible from the divisive influences that may result when teachers are pitted against the superintendent and the board of education in formalized negotiation.

Attempts have been made to cast the superintendent in a variety of roles. Some see him as chief spokesman for the board; others, as a consultant to board members as they do the negotiating. Some view him as consultant both to the board and to teachers; others perceive him as a member of the administrative negotiating team, but not necessarily the chief spokesman—that role being performed by legal counsel or a negotiating specialist.

The issue being raised, though, is whether the superintendent should be the chief negotiator, representing administration and the board. Current negotiation practice offers some clues as to how the superintendent functions in negotiation. The *Negotiation Research Digest* for September 1967, compiled by the Research Division of the National Education Association, indicated that under the provisions of more than 1,500 negotiating agreements:

> *The superintendent performed in negotiating sessions in one of the following roles "negotiator with full authority, negotiator with limited authority, adviser to school board only, adviser to board and teachers, neutral resource person, nonparticipant, and other". . . . Two states, California and Michigan, had model responses which indicate that the superintendent has full authority in negotiation. While these two states have very different negotiation statutes, they also provide almost two-thirds of the "negotiator with full authority" responses. . . . The responses by enrollment strata indicate the influence the various determinants involved in system size may have upon the superintendent's role, in addition to those of legislation. . . . [With enrollments below 50,000] the superintendent's role shifts from that of negotiator with full authority*

to that of adviser to the negotiators for both the teachers and the school board. [2]

Superintendents who function as chief negotiators for their school systems, as a group, strongly believe that it is impossible for the superintendent to serve as "an independent third party." They argue that unless the superintendent is "management" or "the board's man" confusion will reign and that trouble results when he tries to function as adviser to both sides in negotiation. Yet, the *Negotiation Research Digest* data, reported above, indicates that the superintendent is actually functioning as "adviser to the negotiators for both the teachers and the school board" in 41 percent of the instances reported in the 1966–67 NEA survey of written negotiation procedures—by far the most frequently performed role of any that the superintendent assumes.

The problem is that school administrators divide sharply on this issue, and it is difficult, if not impossible, to reconcile these divergencies of belief. Those who favor a labor-management view of negotiation for school systems naturally see the superintendent as "management's representative," i.e., "the board of education's man."

Those who do not adhere to this viewpoint and who strongly believe that the labor-management concept is inappropriate for negotiation in education resist casting the superintendent in an adversary role because it tends to formalize a teacher *vs.* administrator relationship in school administration and weakens the solidarity of effort among all components of personnel in the school system.

What, then, is to be the answer to the question, What should be the superintendent's role in negotiation? His role will be determined by a number of factors. First, his own philosophy toward negotiation and personal preferences will have a major bearing on the role he will assume. Secondly, the board of education may dictate how he will function. Thirdly, state statutes often specify his role. Fourthly, the current climate of teacher-administration relations and the history of those relationships will have a bearing on the matter. A fifth factor may well be the degree to which influence from teacher organizations at the state and national levels is exerted upon the local organization to press for a certain pattern of negotiation procedure.

Today, negotiation in education is done in a variety of ways, and the superintendent is performing his role in no single manner. Therefore, the superintendent will have to judge which role best suits the needs of his school system. He should not hesitate to be the chief negotiator if all of the existing conditions dictate that he should. If they do not, he need not feel he has to conform to a negotiation pattern that is not deemed necessary or appropriate for his situation.

Issue 4

What restrictions, if any, should be put on the scope of negotiation? /In other words, is everything negotiable? Are there no excluded items? This, too, is a moot question. Viewpoints range from no restrictions whatever

[2] National Education Association, Research Division. *Negotiation Research Digest* 1: B-1 to B-7; September 1967.

to very narrow limitations, such as salary and certain fringe benefits.

Some negotiation statutes specify what is negotiable. Teacher organizations tend to press for broadening the scope of negotiation, toward more teacher involvement in decision making—not less. Furthermore, the number of negotiable items tends to increase as negotiation becomes more of an established process.

Many administrators believe certain administrative prerogatives are not negotiable and should be specified in the statute or the agreement, depending on whether negotiation is legally mandated or voluntarily negotiated. This point of view holds that unless these prerogatives are identified and reserved, school administrators and boards of education may find themselves challenged on almost every managerial decision that arises in the operation of the school system.

One approach to determining the scope of negotiation is to make a distinction between *negotiation* and *advisory consultation*. Negotiation is a process wherein the parties come to the negotiating table with divergent points of view about given items and through give-and-take discussion move toward consensus so that agreement may be reached. Items presented for negotiation usually have to do with salary and wage rates, supplemental or fringe benefits, and requests for changes in working conditions that, if granted, clearly have monetary significance. The key to negotiable items is that there is a discernible "asking" and an "offering" price, i.e., a separation of positions at the outset and hopefully a movement toward agreement as negotiation proceeds.

Teachers are insisting that they have a share in determining many other educational decisions concerning policies and procedures in carrying on the instructional program of the school system, matters relating to staff or pupil personnel services, or some phase of business management. The goal is to make the wisest decision possible on the problem under consideration. Since there may or may not be a divergence of viewpoints between teachers and administrators, the problem is how to make the best decision. This may be accomplished by having teachers participate in *advisory consultation*. A standing committee of teachers, administrators, and supervisors would meet regularly throughout the school year and make *advisory recommendations* to the superintendent and board of education.

Advisory consultation is not a new process. Many school systems have used this type of staff involvement for years.

It is quite possible to negotiate those items that should go to the negotiation table and those that would be settled by means of advisory consideration and recommendations. An illustration of this dichotomy follows:

Items for Negotiation	*Items for Advisory Consultation*
1. Revised salary schedule	1. Revision of policies and procedures on teacher assignment and transfer
2. Increased hospitalization benefits	2. Review of leave of absence policies

3. Reduced class size

4. Compensation for committee work

5. Increase in pay scale for summer school teaching and adult education classes

6. Duty-free lunch periods

7. Addition of paraprofessional personnel to give relief from clerical and other nonteaching duties

8. Additional leave for conducting personal business

9. Increase in number of school holidays

10. Terminal leave pay

3. More teacher involvement in textbook selection and curriculum development

4. Greater teacher participation in budget development and allocation of priorities

5. Modification in procedures for handling pupil discipline problems

6. Change in policies governing assignment of student teachers

7. Establishment of a standing advisory committee on staff personnel administration

8. Participation of teachers in reviewing reports of unsatisfactory teacher performance

9. Greater teacher involvement in planning of federally sponsored programs and projects

10. Revision of policies and procedures governing attendance at professional meetings.

In summary, AASA supports the view that a "broadly construed concept of negotiation" makes sense. The broad concept, embracing one stream for formalized negotiation and another for advisory consultation, is suggested as a means for achieving full staff involvement in educational decision making, and AASA draws a distinction between the two by saying "many aspects of public education are appropriate areas for teacher participation. Not all are subject to negotiation." [3]

Issue 5

Should only the parties having ultimate authority for final decision making do the actual negotiating?/The significance of this issue is that it gets at the matter of who should do the negotiating. Some teacher organizations resist negotiating with anyone except the board of education, arguing that it is unproductive to negotiate with the superintendent or his designated representatives because only the board has the authority— legal and otherwise—to implement agreed-upon actions. A logical extension of this point of view would, presumably, even exclude the board of education as a party in negotiation when the board is not fiscally independent. In these situations, negotiation conceivably would take place between the teacher organization and the governmental body that approves school system budgets and levies the taxes required to fulfill their

[3] American Association of School Administrators. *School Administrators View Professional Negotiation.* Washington, D.C.: the Association, 1966. p. 39.

provisions. The extreme possibility would be for negotiation to occur at the state level, since education is a state function and the legislature carries the ultimate responsibility for appropriating a sizable portion of the money for its support.

The "ultimate authority" argument overlooks an important fact, however. The teacher negotiating team, representing the teacher organization, doesn't have "ultimate authority" to act at the negotiation table. It is usually obliged to seek ratification of its tentative agreements. If this is logical for the teacher team, it is equally plausible for the "other side." In fact, the board of education can fulfill its "ultimate authority" role best by delegating to the superintendent and/or his delegated representatives the responsibility for doing the negotiating and holding itself in readiness to ratify or reject the negotiated agreement in the same manner as the teacher organization perceives its responsibility.

There is another valid reason for board members to refrain from direct negotiation. Negotiation is generally believed to be an administrative function. If this is so, board members—as policy makers—should refrain from the operational aspects of negotiation, delegating the function instead to the chief executive of the school system or his designated representatives.

Board members, who are lay citizens contributing their time and effort to public education, already commit a tremendous amount of time to this important public service. To expect them to add to this commitment the additional time required for extended negotiations is unrealistic. Furthermore, it is highly unlikely that most board members are sufficiently familiar with all of the intricate and operational details of the school system to negotiate with complete effectiveness. Equally important, direct negotiation by board members, as pointed out earlier, obscures the function of administration. It blurs the delineation between policy making and administration.

It is true that the money necessary to implement negotiated agreements (contracts) is often approved and appropriated by agencies of government at the county or state level, or both. Negotiators must function within these constraints. There is also the possibility that actions can be taken by teacher organizations in negotiation that will, in turn, exert sufficient public pressure upon boards of education to grant pay increases and other benefits beyond the limits of their capacity to pay. This can and does create crises in school finances. This means that fiscally independent boards of education must communicate carefully to the superintendent the financial constraints that must be taken into account as negotiation proceeds. The board must also be prepared to go to the voters for additional funds if negotiated agreements requiring more money are approved.

When the board of education is fiscally dependent, the need for good communication among the superintendent, his negotiating team, and the board is equally vital. Furthermore, to the extent possible, the board should be aware that its actions may be disapproved by the governmental unit that has fiscal control over its budgetary operations. The consequences of ignoring the need to do so can be costly.

14

In summary, it is believed that negotiation is an administrative function; that direct negotiation should take place between a team representing the teacher organization, recognized for negotiation purposes, and an administrative team established by the superintendent; that the teacher organization can, and likely will, be the ratifying agent for the teacher team; and that the board of education is the ratifying and approving body for the administrative team. This procedure recognizes the validity of the delegation of responsibility and authority principle and the concept of the approving and ratifying power resting in the body either legally or procedurally empowered to so act.

These are but some of the issues that are basic in establishing a perspective toward negotiation. It is readily recognized that not all members of an organization as large and diverse as AASA will concur on every point made. It is also impossible in a publication of this kind to say, with certainty, what the position of AASA is or should be on many of the key issues in negotiation, because only the official resolutions of the Association indicate established policy. The attempt has been only to analyze alternatives, to be sensitive to the fact that there are different approaches to teacher involvement in educational decision making, and that while many variations in procedure exist, there are also many similarities. In addition, it has not seemed feasible to propose a master plan or model for negotiation (were it possible to do so) because we believe that local school systems must design their own plans. AASA's role here has been only to analyze issues, identify trends, and offer general suggestions.

Rationale

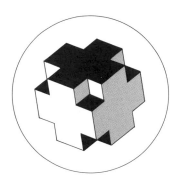

This section is concerned with points of view on attitudes toward negotiation, climate of acceptance or rejection, nature of teacher interests and wants, the public's interest in negotiation, the establishment of state statutes on negotiation, and definition of roles in the process. In addition, definitions of negotiation terms and points of view are listed.

Attitudes Toward Negotiation

There is a considerable range of attitudes toward negotiation, and they often progress through various stages. Three distinct ones are identified here.

Consternation stage./As teachers press for a formalization of the negotiation process, as one or more teacher organizations strive for official recognition, as it becomes obvious that past teacher-administration-board relationships no longer suffice, it is not unusual for administrators and board members to feel a sense of consternation. They are often amazed that teachers should want to abandon informal and presumably pleasant working relationships and insist upon a major modification of those relationships. This development can be unsettling and disturbing; its duration will vary, depending upon the magnitude of the change in working relationships.

Rigidity stage./Consternation may trigger rigidity. Polarized attitudes frequently follow. A hard line of reaction may be adopted on the theory that it is the best defense against aggressive teacher behavior.

In the search for effective negotiating counteractions, administrators and board members may turn to labor-management models in the belief that they will offer the best means for meeting and resisting this manifestation of teacher militancy. Attorneys skilled in collective bargaining procedures or labor relations consultants may be employed to do the negotiating.

Early negotiating sessions often are characterized by considerable rigidity—if not hostility. At best a feeling of uncertainty, due to the newness of the process, may exist. Lack of experience probably accounts for behavior patterns dominated by oversensitivity, defensiveness, and a determination to "save face" at all costs.

Accommodation stage./In time, and as experience is gained, there is usually a mellowing of attitudes; accommodation becomes easier. It becomes less threatening to give in to or to accept criticism from negotiation adversaries. The give-and-take of negotiation becomes better understood, and capability at the negotiation table increases. The temptation to become irritated or angered lessens, frustration is easier to overcome, and negotiating maturity is gradually attained.

Not all school systems go through these stages, but some do. Maturity in negotiation may come about without experiencing consternation and rigidity, but it is important to recognize that varying attitudes toward negotiation often dictate behavior.

Climate for Negotiation

It is easy to misread the meanings of negotiation and draw inaccurate conclusions about its implications. It is true that some administrators and teachers have had negative experiences with negotiation. Those having had these experiences may describe them to colleagues with embellishments. The "grapevine" spreads the word, and the conclusion may be drawn that the same negative experiences will spread to all other school systems and that, sooner or later, all will fall victim to the same unhappy experiences. It is just a matter of time until the uninitiated will find themselves seated across the negotiation table, engaged in verbal battle over an expanding list of items and issues.

On the contrary, if negotiation turns out to be an interesting and positive—if not pleasant—experience, the participants begin to see how it may become a useful process, destined to strengthen staff-administration-board relations. The word may be spread that those who haven't participated in negotiation need not be apprehensive about the prospects.

Neither viewpoint may be entirely accurate or reliable. Negotiation experiences are usually neither totally negative nor completely positive. Thus, to generalize from either extreme is inadvisable.

Climates for acceptance of negotiation differ from community to community and are affected by many factors. If interrelationships in a school system are positive and constructive, the prognosis for successful negotiation is enhanced.

If, on the other hand, relationships are negative and there is a lack of mutual confidence, the chances for successful negotiation are lessened. It is useful to look for evidences of good communication between teacher groups and the administration of the school system. High staff morale is a good sign that the climate for negotiation is favorable. It is helpful, too, to assess the state of mind of teachers and other employees toward their assignments and responsibilities. Evidence of cleavages and discontent in staff relationships should not be underestimated.

POSITIVE INDICATORS

Partnership principle in action./The surest way to tell whether the partnership principle is precept or practice is to see how fully staff members feel involved in decision making. Many school systems claim that teachers and other employees have been and are involved in a wide range of ongoing educational activities. For example, serving on textbook selection committees, being a part of curriculum development projects, functioning on all kinds of advisory committees—at both the local and systemwide levels, helping to initiate new instructional processes, and many other types of involvement may be cited as evidences of the partnership principle in action. This may well be the case.

On the other hand, it is possible for teachers to have had the experience and yet not feel a sense of full partnership. Nominal participation, for whatever the reason, is not peer-level sharing. Somehow the participants must feel that their voices have had equal weight and influence with those of administrators and supervisors if the premise upon which the committee or group was formed was full-partnership involvement.

Open communication./Good communication in all organizations and especially in larger school systems is a perennial problem. Separate offices and divisions have been established to promote both internal and external communication, often with only moderate success. Part of the problem is in the understanding of the word *communication*. It is frequently assumed that it is enough just "to transmit" information from the top downward. A fuller definition of the word, according to Webster, is that it is "a process by which meanings are exchanged between individuals through a common system of symbols."

Open communication means a two-way exchange. Systematic procedures for "feedback" are essential. Another necessary element is the encouragement of free expression of feelings, ideas, and reactions on the part of both parties in the exchange. Traditionally, teachers have been reluctant to freely express themselves to administrators and supervisors. All too often, they have said what they thought the latter wanted to hear—not how they really felt or what they honestly believed. Open communication discourages saying one thing and feeling another.

Cooperative problem solving./One point of view holds that superintendents and their administrative and supervisory assistants are employed to solve educational problems and that teachers should be left free to teach and not be bothered with administrative matters. Some teachers have not only been amenable to this arrangement but have welcomed the "sanctuary" of noninvolvement.

The opposite view is that teachers should have a larger responsibility than classroom instruction per se and that they can make an important contribution toward solving educational problems. When teachers are deeply and intrinsically involved in this process, they will identify with the ongoing goals of the school system; and this may engender a deep sense of professional satisfaction far above that felt by those not having the opportunity or by those electing not to become so involved.

Anticipating or reacting./Problems in the operation of schools are often complicated by the fact that school officials must often react to conditions that have already occurred. An opportunity to anticipate and be better prepared to deal with critical issues is often denied by time and circumstance.

Being behind rather than ahead of problems is a common occurrence. Unfortunately, reactive behavior is made more difficult because the problem solvers must respond not to forces of their own creation but to those that tend to dictate their behavior. Thus, the problem solvers are denied the initiative.

It is preferable to anticipate and identify, as early as possible, those situations and conditions which, if allowed to go unattended, may result in difficult problems. This is easier said than done, but school systems that work hard to achieve this objective usually are better able to surmount problems and survive the rigors of adversity than those that do not. This generalization has special significance in personnel administration, the seedbed for many of the problems that ultimately may become issues for negotiation.

Tolerance for discontent./Strange as it may seem, a tolerance for discontent may be the very safety-valve to prevent normal amounts of employee dissatisfaction from attaining explosive proportions. Some would try to quash discontent in its infancy and "nip in the bud" the views of dissenters before they gain sympathizers and make converts.

Honest dissent is not heresy. In fact, it can be a useful barometer for assessing the temper of employees, especially in large organizations. The school system that provides employees with valid procedures for having their concerns heard and considered without long delays and a great deal of bureaucratic red tape will be in a more favorable position to negotiate with them when the time comes to do so in a formalized manner.

NEGATIVE INDICATORS

Arbitrary administrative action./Fortunately, most school administrators have long since abandoned the use of arbitrary administrative action as the prevailing pattern of leadership behavior. Its complete abandonment, however, hasn't been fully achieved. There are still some school systems in which educational policies, administrative decisions, and operational procedures still are made by the chief school administrator and his close associates. Staff involvement may be minimal—even nonexistent in some cases. A strong personality may succeed, at least for a time, in making most major decisions and determinations and passing them down the line. In time, there will be a reaction, if not in the incumbent's administration, probably in that of his successor. Long doses of arbitrary administrative action build up a backlog of problems and a climate of discontent, and such accumulated dissatisfactions make negotiation more difficult.

Broader staff involvement in decision making has many advantages. Better decisions, more widespread acceptance of decisions, easier implementation of decisions, and greater identity with the ongoing purposes of the school system are a few of the more obvious advantages over arbitrary administrative action.

Delayed corrective action./School administration increases in complexity almost daily, and the number and kinds of problems clamoring for attention multiply rapidly. Establishing problem priorities is a necessity, but it is equally important to evaluate and re-assign priorities from time to time. Perhaps the pressures and volume of work help to explain the delays that sometimes occur in applying appropriate corrective action to personnel problems that may have continued too long.

Undue delay in bringing about needed changes can be costly in terms of the formation of frustrations and attitudes creating tensions that, in turn, may complicate the negotiation process. Since many of the issues that reach the negotiation table arise from personnel problems, it makes a great deal of sense to have an ongoing program that identifies symptoms and assesses their significance early enough to prevent the development of deep-seated problems. Much is done about preventative maintenance in caring for the school plant, but the same care and attention are not given to prevent erosion in human affairs.

Ultrapaternalistic personnel practices./Some school systems with comprehensive and highly sensitive personnel programs have experienced adverse staff reactions, which seems inconsistent with what might be expected as the result of so-called enlightened personnel policies and procedures. The reason for this incongruity may be that the personnel program is too paternalistic.

Motivation has a bearing upon employee attitudes, and the results of the study reported below may offer some clues to the development of good working relations between teachers and school administrators. M. Scott Myers, an industrial psychologist, made a six-year study of employee motivation at Texas Instruments, Inc. In summary, his study showed:

That workers are motivated most effectively by a challenging job which allows a feeling of achievement, responsibility, growth, advancement, enjoyment of work itself, and earned recognition . . . that which dissatisfies workers most are mostly factors which are peripheral to the job—work rules, lighting, coffee breaks, titles, seniority rights, wages, fringe benefits, and the like . . . that workers become dissatisfied when opportunities for meaningful achievement are eliminated and they become sensitized to their environment and begin to find fault.[1]

[1]Myers, M. Scott. "Who Are Your Motivated Workers?" *Harvard Business Review* 42: 73; January-February 1964.

This study and others can guide personnel administrators and super-intendents in developing the kinds of personnel policies and procedures that may motivate employees or smother them with too much paternalism.

Positive and negative indicators of employee attitudes and morale exist in every school system. The task is to be alert to their existence and to recognize their significance as conditioners for negotiation.

Interests Involved in the Negotiation Process

What does negotiation have to do with the public interest? What effect, if any, may it have upon the capacity of the educational enter-prise to provide a level and quality of service commensurate with the public's needs? Does negotiation result in conflicts of interest among the parties concerned and are these of any consequence?

In business and industry, the bargaining parties try to obtain what appears to them to be their fair share of the productivity of the business enterprise. The contending parties, seeking shares of this productivity, are labor and management; management representing the voiced con-cerns of the stockholders; labor, those of the men and women in the work force.

It isn't easy to identify the productivity of the educational enter-prise. The absence of profit-and-loss statements, production records, or levels of dividends to stockholders makes it difficult to assess, in mean-ingful terms, the educational outputs of school systems for negotiation purposes. Some other basis must be found for determining the interests of each of the negotiating parties in education.

The interest of boards of education, of superintendents, of teachers, and of the public need not be incompatible, although it may sometimes appear that they are. After all, negotiation is predicated upon a conflict of interests among the principal parties. Even though frustration and turmoil often characterize the earlier stages of negotiation, time will ameliorate these stresses and strains and greater maturity will result.

It should not be forgotten that three decades ago these same growing pains were felt by labor and management negotiators. Even though the collective bargaining process has never been nor is it now considered to be a "pleasant picnic," stability and maturity in the process have gradu-ally developed. In the course of time, comparable order and stability will prevail in educational negotiation.

Teacher interest./Care has to be exercised in making an accurate assessment of what teachers want and why some of them have become so militant in quest of their desires. The depression of the thirties and its aftereffects in the forties dealt cruelly with teachers. It is doubtful if they were ever more underpaid, overworked, and less appreciated than during World War II. Despite these conditions, they endured their hard-ships quietly with little or no protest. Why, then, do they protest so vehemently today when so many changes for the better have been made in their compensation, working conditions, and status? Something new has been added.

Some believe that "something new" is a keener awareness of the link between the state of one's education and the state of his economic well-being. The economic health of our society depends upon better educated citizens. None knows this better than parents—who are determined to see that their children get the kind and quality of education that provides economic advantages and security.

Thus, teachers are now accorded a level of power hardly dreamed of in the thirties, forties, and fifties. Teachers as a group now only have to indicate their displeasure, and immediately their actions have effects upon the economic well-being of the community. When a cessation of teaching services is threatened or actually occurs, apprehension grips the parents of the school district. This is the new-found power that teachers are exerting in the quest for higher salaries, more supplemental benefits, and better conditions of work. They have always had plenty of wants; now they are getting the power to do something about them.

Teachers want higher salaries and a greater share in determining the educational policies and procedures that affect their work. The attainment of these objectives will result, they say, in a higher level of teaching service, thereby raising the quality of education. They have tried to gain these objectives in various ways. For years, they were content to leave to the superintendent and the board of education all determinations in these areas. Gradually, committees of teachers—usually the salary committee—met with the superintendent and the board to present requests, but not to negotiate. They had to be content with the decisions made by the administration and board.

Now the pattern of participation is changing to that of negotiation. Whether it is the most effective means to obtain the ends sought is a question about which there is considerable difference of opinion. However, the trend toward negotiation is growing, even as the debate on its desirability continues.

Whether rivalry between NEA-affiliated teacher associations and the AFL-CIO–oriented AFT was a cause or a result of teacher unrest is open to question. Nevertheless, contests for the right to represent and speak for teachers in staff participation with superintendents and boards of education raised the priority of negotiation among the concerns of school administrators.

Perhaps the pressure of teachers to insist upon an unlimited agenda in negotiation reflects an accumulation of needs and wants built up over more than three decades. The task now is to re-evaluate what teachers need and require. Keener awareness of their expectations may help to expedite negotiation. Sensing which items on the agenda are of primary and which are of peripheral concern is extremely important.

The following are some prime reasons for teacher dissatisfaction and for their increased militancy:

- Discontent with traditional methods of teacher involvement in educational decision making.
- Mounting class sizes and crowded classroom space.
- Social change, pupil mobility, racial unrest, and concurrent changes, especially in urban communities.
- Necessity to "moonlight" to make ends meet.
- Frustration with traditional instructional methods and materials,

which clearly do not meet the needs of pupils having learning difficulties.
- Insensitive administrative procedures and overpaternalistic personnel practices.
- Cleavages between teacher groups and contests for organizational power and status.
- Increase in number of new teachers coming from labor-union families and backgrounds.
- Increased educational level of teaching staff.
- Increased awareness of recent research on personnel practices.
- Reaction against oversupervision or inappropriate supervision.

Underlying the tangible needs and desires of teachers, as indicated by the number and kinds of items included on negotiation lists, are some less tangible factors. In describing the role of the teacher in relation to the authority structure of the school, Norman J. Boyan stresses some factors that underlie their needs and wants. Teachers, says Boyan—

have become more expert . . . have found new strength in their local organizations . . . have been encouraged by new patterns of public and private support for continuous technical upgrading to look more to their colleague group than to their hierarchical superordinates as relevant reference groups . . . have begun to take seriously the exhortation . . . to participate more vigorously in local educational decision making . . . have launched the search for a new pattern of teacher-administrator relations.[2]

Reduced to the simplest terms, teachers want to be recognized as important partners in the resolution of important educational decisions. They feel they have a particular kind of expertise to offer in the solution of educational problems. They aren't satisfied just "to be briefed" after decisions have been made; they want to be involved at the outset of determinations.

Teacher desires and demands may seem excessive and unreasonable, especially during the period of adjustment when the parties are trying to become accustomed to the newness of the process and when one party may be testing the strength of the other. At such times it is tempting to flex muscles and develop rigid attitudes, but the meaning of the inflexibilities should not be misjudged. Time tends to ameliorate tautness and gradually more realistic positions will be assumed by both parties.

Some teacher negotiating groups present extensive requests. Tactically, they may present these requests in a manner and with an intensity calculated to throw their adversaries on the defensive. The strategy used may parallel some of the procedures that labor unions have used successfully in bargaining with management. This approach may tempt board members and school administrators to become disillusioned at what may seem to be irresponsible tactics. Another reaction may be to develop "a hard line" and resist all pressure to retreat from it. While such approaches to negotiation result in tension, acrimony, and frustration, many teacher groups make reasonable requests both in nature and

[2]Allen, Roy B., and Schmid, John, editors. *Collective Negotiations and Educational Administration.* Columbus, Ohio: University Council for Educational Administration, 1966. pp. 18-20.

number. They recognize that responsible negotiation imposes self-restraints and self-discipline, although this is not to say that they present themselves as "soft pushovers" inclined to compromise on every issue.

The point is that negotiation is a relatively new process in teacher-board-administration relations. Those who are involved as negotiators are "feeling their way." Excesses will occur, but they must be put in proper perspective. Premature conclusions that calamitous days have fallen upon staff-administrative-board relations should be resisted.

It is very important to assess what teachers want, to attempt to distinguish between basic and peripheral requests, to refrain from becoming unduly defensive, to seek for areas of agreement rather than for points of conflict, and even to be somewhat indulgent of irrational and emotional behavior. These reactions to wants of teachers are calculated to bring more maturity in negotiation and a greater promise of stability than if one yields to the temptation to "fight fire with fire."

Teachers believe that it is in the public interest to press for a higher level of expenditures for public education inasmuch as this will more nearly assure quality education. They believe also that a new look needs to be taken at the way administrative and managerial decisions are made and that they should have a share in the making of many of these decisions.

Administration interest./The interest of the administrator in negotiation—especially the superintendent—is to work for balanced support of all educational components, i.e., to strive for a fair and equitable allocation of funds to support the total educational enterprise.

An additional concern of the superintendent is to keep the day-to-day, orderly processes of education functioning without undue interruptions and work stoppages. The possibility of strikes and sanctions being called in the case of negotiation impasses makes this a more difficult and demanding responsibility.

The superintendent and his administrative and supervisory staff have the responsibility for providing the professional and technical leadership required to enable schools to achieve their purposes. The superintendent is largely responsible for staff procurement; for initiating administrative and supervisory procedures that will facilitate good instruction; for securing the best possible facilities, equipment, and supplies necessary to carry out the instructional program; and for coordinating all the components of the educational enterprise.

The administrative interest in negotiation is not chiefly to deny teachers their legitimate needs and demands. In fact, most superintendents recognize that higher teacher salaries, increased fringe benefits, and improved working conditions make the school system a more attractive place to work. Thus, staff recruitment is usually facilitated and holding power increased. However, the superintendent must be mindful, in negotiation, that other components also need to be maintained at sufficiently high levels of effectiveness to achieve quality education.

Board of education interest./There are some who would draw a direct parallel between negotiation and collective bargaining insofar as the public interest in education is concerned. This parallelism would relate the following roles as follows:

Negotiation	Collective Bargaining
Public	= Stockholders
Board of Education	= Board of Directors
Superintendent	= Chief Negotiator
Teachers	= Labor

This parallelism is based upon the premise that the labor-management concept can and should be applied to education. However, many school administrators reject this assumption, arguing that to do so not only oversimplifies the situation, but assumes comparisons that aren't necessarily valid. The logic supporting this rejection has already been stated in an earlier section and need not be repeated here.

In negotiation, as conceived in this publication, the board of education is seen as the agency most directly responsible to the public. The board must safeguard the public's interest in its schools. This does not mean that teachers should not be concerned about keeping schools strong and capable of meeting the continuing requirements of society. Superintendents, too, are conscious of the public's interest in education. Yet the board of education has to answer *directly* to the public for its actions in the management of schools as these actions are affected by negotiation.

Public interest./The public's interest in its schools has been well stated by AASA in pointing out that "the schools serve not only individuals as such, but the totality of society as well—society with its ideals, its values, its purposes, its commitments, its institutions, its enterprises, its governmental processes. . . . "[3] Another measure of the public's interest in public education is the level of its financial support of its schools. Five years ago, the estimated expenditures for elementary and secondary schools were about $21.1 billion. The amount had risen to $26.3 billion in 1966–67. The projection for 1970 is $43.4 billion.

The public's interest is to see that the quality of education is kept as high as possible and that it is responsive to the requirements of all children. This interest has a three-fold aspect. The first is to provide a level of support commensurate with requirements for national growth and development. The second is to improve the quality of existing programs of education, and the third is to safeguard the investment already made in the educational establishment. Stewardship of the public's interest in education, as has already been pointed out, is vested in boards of education.

Whether the public's interest in its schools is judged in qualitative or quantitative terms, it is clear that whatever improves the quality of educational service is in the public interest and that which detracts from its effectiveness puts that interest in jeopardy. Thus, the public's interest in negotiation must not be minimized at the negotiation table. This places an obligation upon all parties to remember that *means* are as important as *ends*.

In the thrust for greater economic security and a broader involvement in educational decision making, teachers may feel compelled to

[3]American Association of School Administrators. *Imperatives in Education.* Washington, D.C.: the Association, 1966. p. 2.

assume a harsh and aggressive posture. Self-interest appears to supersede all other considerations. The interests of children and the public may appear to be secondary concerns. This type of behavior often evokes resistance from board members and school administrators. Even public antipathy may be generated.

The first and foremost responsibility is to children. Inflexible positions taken by negotiators often lead to impasses; these, in turn, may result in work stoppages by whatever name called—strikes, sanctions, sick days, professional days, or withdrawals of service—and add up to one result, namely, loss of instructional services to children. The public's interest is impaired when *any means* are used to achieve the ends desired.

Having cautioned against a disregard of the public's interest, it is important to add that the public must also fulfill its obligation to education. It must be willing to provide sufficient levels of support to enable school systems to pay salaries, grant fringe benefits, and provide working conditions which will attract and hold highly qualified personnel. Boards of education and school administrators must also perceive their responsibilities as being more than just "efficient managers," reluctant to share with staff members, in a meaningful manner, educational decisions of common concern.

The Law and Negotiation

The number of states that have enacted laws governing negotiation is gradually increasing. As of the summer of 1967, 15 states—Alaska, California, Connecticut, Florida, Massachusetts, Michigan, Minnesota, Nebraska, New Hampshire, New York, Oregon, Rhode Island, Texas, Washington, Wisconsin—had passed statutes. New Jersey has a resolution on the subject. The major impetus for enacting statutes on negotiation usually can be traced to pressure for action on the part of employee groups and organizations.

Michigan's legislation most nearly parallels the labor-management model. Wisconsin's statute also has many of the same similarities. Such legislation creates problems for public education because it is based upon the hypothesis that the conditions prevailing in business and industry exactly parallel those in education. Most school administrators and students of the negotiation process are persuaded that there are enough unique qualities about public education to justify special legislation fitted to its requirements, rather than to include it in statutes of broader application. Often, the labor orientation of the latter type of law makes it necessary to separate administrative-supervisory personnel from teachers.

The recognition that the labor-management collective bargaining process is not particularly appropriate for public schools has prompted teachers associations and school administrators associations, in the states not having such legislation, to collaborate in drafting bills that may prove to be more suitable for educational institutions. Boards of education frequently join in these endeavors. Teachers unions, on the other hand, have no aversion to laws patterned on the labor-management format, for obvious reasons.

Advisability of statutes./The desirability of legalizing negotiation has been warmly debated in educational circles. While more and more states are moving toward enactments, many others show little inclination, at the present time, to push for such legislation.

There are some who argue that state laws on negotiation merely institutionalize employer-employee conflict in schools. They are not opposed to the formation of procedures to conduct negotiation, but believe it better to enter into these agreements and arrangements voluntarily, without the compulsion of law. They further argue that laws tend to be fashioned upon the labor-management format more often than not, even though the legislation is drawn primarily for schools.

There is another side to the coin, however. State laws appropriate to the requirements of school systems do provide a framework for conducting negotiations. If the provisions of the statute are kept reasonably flexible, local school systems have guidelines to follow in their formalized relationships with their employees. This can be helpful to large and small school systems alike. Rigid laws, however, are not helpful.

The trend toward more state legislation on negotiation is well established, and more laws will be enacted. This being the case, it would seem desirable to profit by the experiences of others and seek to fashion new statutes as carefully as possible to bring rationality and stability to the negotiation process. From this point of view, it makes sense to have good laws "on the books." Public policy has, for three decades, favored orderly processes in labor-management relations. Legislation has, generally speaking, promoted better employee-employer relations. It is probable that public policy may also dictate the formation of formalized procedures for enabling teachers to be more responsively involved in educational decision making. If this is so, then it follows that state statutes on negotiation may be quite beneficial.

Content of state laws./An examination of the negotiation laws already enacted reveals great variance in their scope and substance. The Alaska law, for example, is a very general enabling statute making it possible for the state or a political subdivision of the state to "enter into a contract with a labor organization whose members furnish services to the state or the political subdivision."[4] The California and Michigan laws, on the other hand, go into great detail, prescribing negotiation procedures in a very comprehensive manner.

In general, however, the more comprehensive laws contain sections that govern the following basic elements in negotiation:

1. *Definitions.* Terms are explained and clarified. Most statutes contain a preamble, containing not only definitions but the purposes to be served by the law.

2. *Right of membership in professional organizations.* The rights of teachers and other school employees to join the professional organization of their choice are specified.

3. *Prohibitions against coercion.* A provision sometimes exists that definitely prohibits any kind of coercive action on the part of the em-

[4]Alaska Statutes, 1962. Title 23, sec. 23.40.010—23.40.030.

ploying organization (school system) against individuals or groups who have formed an association to engage in negotiation.

4. *Ascertaining majority organization.* Methods may be stipulated to determine the organization(s) that will represent the employees in negotiation. If elections are to be the determining method, their frequency is usually indicated.

5. *Rights of "minority" groups.* Provisions often are made to ensure that groups not representing the majority of employees also have opportunities to make requests and to be heard by the employing organization (board of education).

6. *Right of negotiation.* The right of the representatives of the organization chosen to represent the majority of employees to negotiate with the employing agency or organization is indicated.

7. *Composition of "negotiating unit."* Stipulations are made as to the composition of the "negotiating unit," with indications of who may and may not be represented by the unit.

8. *"Good faith" negotiation.* The elements of "good faith" negotiation are specified.

9. *Conditions conducive to negotiation.* Specifications for the employing organization to observe are listed describing reasonable conditions for scheduling negotiation sessions and other contacts with employees.

10. *Resolution of impasses.* Provisions—which may or may not be quite detailed and complete—are made for resolving negotiation impasses.

11. *Mediation, conciliation, and arbitration.* Some states have provision for mediating, conciliating, or arbitrating the disputes on which the negotiating parties cannot reach agreement. These procedures may be used to resolve impasses. (See Item 10.)

12. *Fact finding.* In some instances, fact-finding procedures are stipulated when disputes appear incapable of resolution.

13. *Unfair labor practices.* Recourses against unfair labor practices may be specified, especially in those states with laws fashioned along labor-management lines.

14. *No-strike provision.* In most instances, specific prohibition against strikes and work stoppages is included in the law.

15. *Agreements and contracts.* Authorization to consummate an agreement or contract, with some indication of its duration, often is provided for.

16. *Re-opening of negotiation.* The period of time during which negotiation may not be re-opened is sometimes specified and the conditions indicated under which re-opening discussions may be conducted.

The above 16 elements in negotiation statutes are illustrations of the type of provision made in such laws. Legalistic language often makes it necessary for school systems to have the advice and guidance of legal counsel and explains why more systems are considering having this type of technical service available on a continuing basis.

The NEA Research Division has published a legal analysis and review that provides a more comprehensive treatment of the "legal status of the teaching profession's negotiation with school boards, the types of statutes which presently operate in this field, and the kind of legislation which would be necessary to require boards to meet with representatives of their employees."[5]

As more negotiation laws are enacted, negotiators must become fully knowledgeable of the law and avoid its violation both in letter and in spirit. This makes observance of legal requirements of top-level importance. A sound negotiation law, as earlier indicated, can be quite useful in that it reduces the limits for dispute in carrying out the negotiation process. On the other hand, laws do require negotiators to be fully informed about what can and cannot be done. One important implication of this fact is that negotiation not only is becoming a more formalized process but demands a level of expertise that almost dictates that negotiators become "specialists" in the art of negotiation.

Two Approaches to Negotiation

Before attempting to define the roles of those who will be involved in negotiation, it may be useful to consider two different methods of conducting teacher-administrator-board of education dialogue.

While negotiation has spread rapidly in recent years in many states, it still is not the predominant process for making educational decisions. This means that many school systems do not have to accept negotiation as the only method for involving teachers and other staff members in this important process. Thus, it is a mistake to minimize less formal procedures for decision making.

For many years, hundreds of school systems have deliberately involved teachers in a responsible manner in determining a wide range of educational decisions. This involvement has been genuine and not just an exercise in superficiality.

This is not to argue that all school systems have been dedicated to the continued involvement of teachers in decision making. The rapid rise of negotiation testifies to this fact. Neither is it being argued that teachers will not press for more formalized negotiation procedures in those systems that now use more informal techniques.

The two contrasting approaches for making educational determinations can best be described by the two diagrams that follow. The first may be termed *around the table consultation*. The second may be called *across the table negotiation*. The former is an informal process, stressing cooperative participation of all parties concerned. The latter is more an adversary-type, "give-and-take" process, moving from divergence to consensus or impasse if agreement cannot be reached. The former avoids many problems that must be resolved in negotiation, e.g., determining who shall be represented in the negotiation unit, defining the role of the superintendent, deciding what is negotiable, agreeing upon rules of negotiation, deciding what to do in case of impasse, and so on. Another major difference between the two processes is that negotiation tends to divide the profession into conflicting components and destroys the unity that is regarded by many as essential to the welfare of the educational enterprise.

[5]National Education Association, Research Division. *Professional Negotiation with School Boards*. Research Report 1965-R3. Washington, D.C.: the Association, March 1965. p. 5.

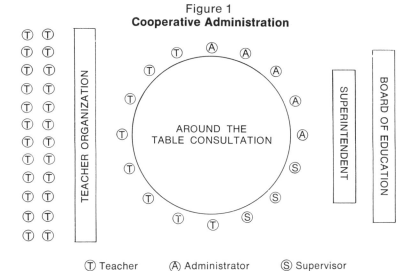

Figure 1
Cooperative Administration

Ⓣ Teacher   Ⓐ Administrator   Ⓢ Supervisor

1. *Identification of problems and issues*
2. *Presentation of evidence and arguments*
3. *Give-and-take discussion*
4. *Peer-level participation*
5. *Reaching consensus*
6. *Formulation of recommendations*

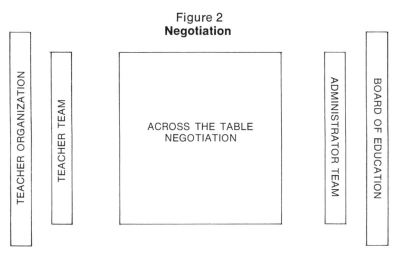

Figure 2
Negotiation

1. *Presentation of proposals (demands)*
2. *Submission of counter proposals*
3. *Pro-and-con arguments*
4. *Presentation of evidence and supportive data*
5. *Employment of tactics and strategies*
6. *Reaching consensus or impasse*
7. *Signing an agreement (contract) or resolving an impasse*

Cooperative administration is predicated upon the belief that teachers and other staff members should be directly involved in a wide variety of educational determinations. Perhaps the most obvious and most common form of consultation is that of having committees of teachers discuss areas of concern with the superintendent and/or his designated representatives, and to make recommendations to the board of education.

Standing teacher committees that advise and counsel the superintendent and his staff are quite common and assist school administrators in many useful and valuable ways.

Many ad hoc teacher committees study curriculum development, instructional improvement, textbook selection, course of study formation, and problem solving of all kinds and develop or review personnel policies and procedures. Thousands of teachers have engaged in these endeavors with profit to themselves and to the school system itself.

Teacher organizations may or may not designate individual teachers to serve on committees. Sometimes, lists of nominees are presented to the superintendent or his staff. Selections are then made from these lists. The point is that, in this form of consultation, teachers do not have to be "hand picked" or dominated by administrators. Consultation does not have to be a superficial process wherein teachers are merely figureheads dominated by their administrative and supervisory counterparts.

The superintendent is able to form composite committees of teachers, administrators, and supervisors to join him in making decisions on a wide range of topics and problems. All members sit as peers. Their interests can be carefully considered as problems are resolved. The ultimate objective, however, is to reach a decision that will best serve the interests of all parties and one that may be best for the school system as a whole.

This type of staff involvement in educational decision making is in use in many school systems across the country. Perhaps one of the most successful is the "6+6 plan" in operation in the Memphis Public Schools, Memphis, Tennessee. This plan not only is an example of an effective alternative to negotiation but demonstrates a form of teacher-administrator-board relationships that avoids many of the divisive problems inherent in negotiation.

The Memphis model is just one example of an option in interstaff relations open to school administrators; other approaches are being suggested, as was pointed out by Metzler and Knade in a recent issue of the *American School Board Journal.*[6]

Negotiation./The rate at which formalized negotiation has become the accepted method of decision making in school systems is rapidly accelerating. Pressure from many teacher organizations to supplant informal consultatory procedures with this more formalized process has caused an increasing number of school administrators to seek more knowledge of and skill in negotiation. In response to this need, more publications on the subject are appearing, and many inservice training activities are being organized.

Negotiation is basically an adversative process. It places teachers,

[6]Metzler, John H., and Knade, Oscar, Jr. "A Tranquilizer for Negotiations." *American School Board Journal* 155: 12-13; December 1967.

through their organizational representatives, across the negotiation table from school administrators, who represent the board of education.

Proposals (demands) are presented; counterproposals may be offered; arguments with supportive data are given; points of view may be challenged; concessions, on both sides of the table, may be made; consensus or disagreement may follow; an agreement (contract) may be signed; or an impasse may result. If the latter occurs, some form of resolving the impasse must be found. These are the elements of negotiation. The parties usually start with differing points of view and hopefully work toward closing the gap.

While negotiation is predicated upon an adversative principle, it does not necessarily have to be a negative process. It simply is a different method for making educational decisions and determinations. It is often new and unfamiliar; it puts teachers and administrators in new kinds of roles. If conducted badly, it can be a disruptive process; if carried out skillfully, it may be as productive as more familiar and traditional procedures by which teachers, administrators, and board members reach agreements and solve problems.

Participants./Who are the individuals who will be involved in negotiation? Generally speaking, they fall into two classifications—one representing teachers; the other, the administration and the board of education. An examination of existing pacts providing for negotiation between teacher organizations and the officials of school systems indicates that there is no uniform pattern for conducting negotiation and the roles of the participants may vary, depending upon the pattern used. Despite these differences in negotiation structure, there is more commonality in role performance than might be supposed. This makes it possible to draw some conclusions about definition of roles in negotiation and to suggest some models for conducting the process.

Before suggesting some different negotiation models and the roles various individuals may perform, it may be useful to consider modifications in attitudes of the participants as they perform their roles in negotiation.

Initial impact period./When it becomes apparent that past or even existing teacher-administrator-board relationships are no longer adequate and teachers press for the formalization of the negotiation process, some administrators and board members feel uncomfortable and apprehensive. They may even express surprise and disappointment that teachers should want to reject informal working relationships in favor of negotiation. This readjustment in relationships often creates a climate of uncertainty and confusion, the duration of which varies depending upon the magnitude of the change.

Rigidity period./A common reaction to the teachers' demand for negotiation is for administrators and board members to respond rigidly to the demand. Attitudes may get polarized, and a hard line of reaction is considered as the most appropriate way to counteract aggressive teacher behavior.

Earlier negotiating sessions may be very formal, strained, and, in some cases, hostile. The newness of the process, unfamiliarity with the techniques of negotiation, and a general feeling of uncertainty often make this a trying time.

Adjustment period./The second and third rounds of negotiation usually are easier than the first. Time and experience tend to remove tension. The negotiating parties become more sure of themselves; accommodations are more easily made. The give-and-take nature of negotiation becomes better understood. Defensiveness becomes less apparent; the need to "save face," less necessary.

Acceptance period./Once negotiation becomes an accepted process in teacher-administrator-board relationships, refinements are usually made in the structure and strategies of negotiation, all of which help to make it a more mature and stable process. Negotiation thus can take its place among other more traditional administrative processes.

Negotiation Models

Negotiation, generally, is considered to be a bilateral, adversary-type process, with teacher representatives on one side and administrative-supervisory-board of education members on the other. Each of the following has a role in the negotiation process:

Teachers	*Administrator–Board Members*
1. Individual teachers	1. Board of education members
2. Leaders of teacher organizations	2. Superintendent
3. Members of negotiating team	3. Department and division heads
4. Team leader (chief spokesman)	4. Principals and supervisors
5. Consultants	5. Consultants
6. Legal counsel	6. Legal counsel
7. State and national teacher organization representatives	

Before defining the roles of each of the above individuals or groups, consideration must be given to some models for negotiation. These models apply to *across the table negotiation* rather than to *around the table consultation.* No attempt is being made to prescribe these models as the only ones that might be used in negotiation. They are suggestions only and should be so considered. Their applicability will depend on factors that only local school officials can assess.

Model I

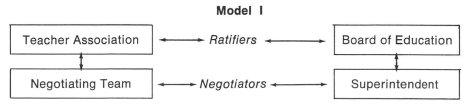

Model I./This is a simple format for negotiation wherein the teacher association and the board of education are the ratifying bodies. The teacher team and the superintendent do the actual negotiating, the latter as the board's delegated representative.

The characteristics of this model are that it (a) puts the superintendent in a crucial position of having to do the negotiating by himself, (b) may cause him to feel that the "adversary role" as negotiator jeopardizes his other working relationships with teachers, and (c) requires a commitment in terms of time, effort, and expertise that he may find difficult to fulfill.

Two advantages of this model are that it is easy to understand and that it keeps policy making and administration from becoming confused. It does, however, put the superintendent on the so-called "management side" of the table, and some chief school executives deplore casting negotiation in this labor-management format. This model also presumes that the superintendent has the knowledge, skill, and temperament to be an able negotiator or that he can develop them. This may or may not be a valid assumption.

Model II

Teacher Association	←→ Ratifiers ←→	Board of Education
		Superintendent
Negotiating Team	←→ Negotiators ←→	Professional Negotiator

Model II./The main difference between Model I and Model II is that in Model II a professional negotiator is employed by the board of education to do the actual negotiating. The superintendent is the liaison representative between the board and the professional negotiator. He provides the data and information that the negotiator will need; he consults with both the board and the negotiator; he may or may not attend all negotiating sessions; he provides the educational expertise that the professional negotiator needs. The professional negotiator may or may not be a lawyer; his primary expertise is in negotiation.

This model has these advantages: (a) it has a reasonably simple format, as does Model I; (b) it permits the superintendent to be closely involved in negotiation but does not force him into the role of chief negotiator if he finds that position distasteful or if he does not feel himself well suited to that position; and (c) it keeps the board of education in the role of ratifier.

The disadvantages of this type of negotiation are that (a) it reflects the "labor-management" format, (b) it still puts the superintendent on the "management side of the table," and (c) it assumes an ample supply of "professional negotiators," an assumption that probably is not valid.

Model III./This model resembles Model I, except that the superintendent forms an administrative team to negotiate with the teacher team. He serves as chairman, however.

The advantages of Model III are that (a) it is easily understood, i.e., roles are clear-cut; (b) the "team" idea introduces a concept of

34

Model III

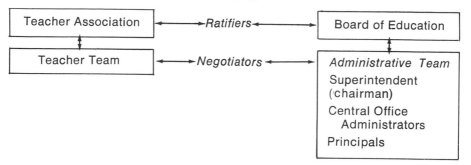

involvement of other administrators (including principals), thus giving the superintendent assistance and support; (c) it provides balance in negotiation, i.e., a teacher team and an administrative team are pitted opposite each other.

Its disadvantages are the same as those of Model II in that, unless proper effort is made, it tends to intensify the divisive characteristics of a labor-management type of negotiation.

While the above model shows the superintendent as chairman of the administrative team, that role could be performed by some other team member. In fact, another advantage of Model III is that it enables the superintendent to perform in the capacity best suited to his desires and capabilities.

Model IV

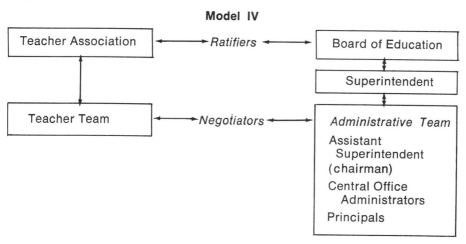

Model IV./The difference between this model and Model III is that the superintendent designates one of his assistant superintendents as chief negotiator. This, of course, presumes a system large enough to have assistant superintendents. It avoids the necessity of putting the superintendent in that role whether or not he wishes to be so cast. Systems large enough to use this format probably demand so much of the superintendent's time and attention that he would find it difficult to give the time required to conduct negotiation.

35

It would be difficult to say that one of the above models is markedly superior to the others. School systems must tailor their negotiation procedures in accordance with the restrictions within which they have to work and within the capabilities of their own administrative and supervisory personnel.

Model V

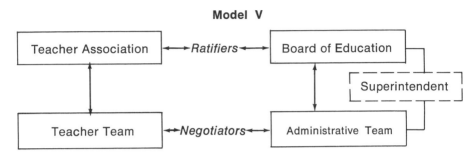

Model V./This model places the superintendent in the role of consultant to the board and the administrative team. The latter may be made up of designated representatives on the superintendent's staff, with one of the team assigned the role of chief spokesman. The advantage of this arrangement is that it enables the superintendent to be very close to the policy makers (board members) and the negotiators but does not oblige him to be committed as deeply, in terms of time and effort. The superintendent functions as the "coach," and the chief spokesman of the administrative team functions as the "team captain."

Participation in Negotiation

Teachers./Among the teacher participants in negotiation are the individual teachers themselves. Teachers participate through their representatives at the negotiation table. They have the right to join the professional organization of their choice and to designate it to be their sole representative in negotiation. This choice must be free and open and must include the privilege of refraining from designating any organization to represent them if they do not wish to join any association or union.

Leaders of teacher organizations./The duly elected officers or other designated leaders of the organization chosen to represent the majority of the teachers should be recognized as the spokesmen with whom the administration and/or board will work in establishing the "ground rules" under which negotiation will be conducted.

These leaders may or may not serve on the teacher team that conducts the actual negotiation. This will depend upon such factors as the availability of other teachers who may have skill as negotiators, the wishes of the leaders themselves, and the policies of the association regarding the function of the officers of the organization.

Members of the teachers' negotiating team./The teachers chosen by the teacher organization conduct the "case" for the teachers as a whole. The number on the team varies as do the methods for determining who will serve on the team. Members of the negotiating team are beginning to develop skills in the art of negotiation. One state education association, in a manual prepared for teacher groups and commended for use by the association, lists several characteristics that might be used as criteria for selecting teacher negotiators. If a teacher develops the qualities these criteria stipulate, he would "recognize and react to subtle nuances of the dialogue of negotiation . . . have an acute sense of timing . . . judge when an aggressive or forceful posture is indicated and when a more reserved approach will gain the advantage."[7]

Team leader (chief spokesman)./There is some difference of opinion about the advisability of designating one person on the team as chief spokesman. The advantage of having a chairman of the team is that there is better coordination and less danger of making comments or statements that may be detrimental to the progress of negotiation.

The disadvantage of having a chief spokesman is that he would have to carry a heavy load in the negotiation dialogue. Furthermore, as other members of the team gain skill in negotiation, they will not be able to contribute directly.

Consultants./Generally speaking, consultants are those staff specialists—general administrators, instructional supervisors, research directors, fiscal officials—within the school system who have special knowledge or expertness that the negotiators may need or find useful. The consultant may be called upon to react to proposals negotiated from the point of view of his particular area or specialization and may give his opinions either outside of or during the negotiation sessions.

Individuals outside the system may also participate in negotiation. Lawyers skilled in negotiation procedure may be needed to make certain that the process is conducted according to law (if statutes apply) or to agreed-upon procedures.

Another type of consultant is one who represents a national, regional, or state education organization whose advice and counsel is sought by the teachers' negotiation team. This sort of consultation is usually directed toward some aspect of the negotiating process itself.

Legal counsel./Legal counsel may be used by both negotiating teams. One caution is especially important: Legal counsel must have expertise in negotiation. The legal counsel traditionally employed by the board of education may not be qualified for this specialized responsibility because the tasks customarily performed by these board of education attorneys are quite different from the requirements of negotiators.

Legal counsel may be used either as chief negotiator or as an adviser to the chief negotiator and members of the administrative team.

Teacher organizations may obtain the services of legal counsel either to advise on the general conduct of the negotiation or to counsel the teacher team members on the substantive issues under consideration. As state laws on negotiation become more widespread and prescriptive, legal counsel can be useful in making sure that negotiation proceeds legally and that the text of agreements (contracts) is properly stated.

---

[7]Law, Kenneth L., and others. *The Manual for Teacher Negotiators.* Windsor, Conn.: Educational Consultative Services, 1966. p. 2.

State and national teacher organization representatives./Teacher organizations at the state and national levels are concerning themselves more and more with negotiation. They are increasing their field assistance to local teacher organizations by providing inservice training, direct counsel and advice, and other kinds of support. This trend is likely to increase, and it causes many administrators to wonder whether such field service should be restricted to teachers only or whether it should also be extended to school administrators, since many of them are members of the same organizations as the teachers at both the state and national levels (e.g., state education associations and NEA).

Board of education members./It has already been indicated that individual board members best serve as policy makers and ratifiers of the actions agreed upon by their designated negotiator(s). Implicit in this definition of role is the belief that negotiation is an administrative function and, as such, is best performed by school administrators rather than board members. What applies to individual board members also seems appropriate for the entire board functioning as a committee of the whole.

Superintendent./Perhaps, the best that can be said is that the superintendent should be responsible for seeing that negotiation is conducted as an administrative function. His own role may be any of the following:

1. Chief negotiator, representing the board
2. Member of the administrative negotiating team, but not its chief spokesman
3. Consultant to board and administrative team
4. Consultant to an "outside" negotiator designated to conduct negotiations for the board.

When negotiation is conducted between teacher representatives and board members, the superintendent may function as a consultant for both groups. However, this role is more common in "around-the-table" administrative consultation than in "across-the-table" negotiation.

Department and division heads./At this level, administrators and supervisors function primarily in an advisory capacity to the superintendent. They help him analyze the implications of negotiation requests and advise him as to the probable educational consequences of granting specific items. They may, from time to time, attend negotiating sessions as consultants, answering questions and giving reactions as the occasion requires.

Principals and supervisors./Principals and supervisors are concerned about their appropriate roles in negotiation. Are they to be an integral part of the process or "bystanders" who wonder what is going on and who feel apprehensive about its results? Principals may be more directly concerned than supervisory personnel because of their day-to-day responsibilities at the local school level. That supervisors are keenly concerned is carefully pointed out in a recent publication of the Association for Supervision and Curriculum Development:

> *Professional negotiations may well mean the end of the tight rope act performed by the supervisor and the curriculum worker who walked*

carefully between ideas and teachers, between teachers and administrators, between administrative imperative and staff consensus, who walked gingerly down the dotted lines for the most part knowing that full lines existed around him. It may well mean that the supervisor or the curriculum director has to declare the camp within which he will work; that he has to declare the methodology that he will pursue. The spin-off from some such considerations will, in fact, affect the negotiation process as well as the planning and deciding processes in the near future. The question may well become: is the supervisor or the designated curriculum worker to be aligned with the superintendent and his administrative staff, or with the teacher and his supportive staff? Thus role definition, which has always been a difficult question, may well be resolved in terms of the negotiation process or resolved on the basis of certain levels of decision-making.[8]

If the principal and supervisor function as "bystanders," they will have minimum involvement in the negotiation process—perhaps none at all. They may be aware of the items being negotiated. Their advice may be sought on the implications of the requests or on the advisability of granting them. They may even attend some negotiating sessions as observers or to answer specific questions. This type of peripheral involvement, however, is more incidental than planned. The "bystander" role frequently engenders insecurity. The principal often wonders if his position is becoming expendable or if his leadership prerogatives are being endangered.

If, on the other hand, principals and supervisors become active "participators" in negotiation, their involvement becomes more responsible. Planned participation involves systematic review of items on the negotiation list; careful analysis of the administrative and instructional implications of certain items; and estimations of the consequences of granting or rejecting these items.

If principals and supervisors are represented on the negotiating team (probably the administrative team), they will be enabled to follow the negotiation process step by step. Admittedly, this casts them in the role of being "across the table" from the teacher team; and not all principals and supervisors may wish to be so identified, feeling that it may alienate them from teachers. However, this basic decision cannot be made solely by principals and supervisors themselves.

If representatives of principals and supervisors participate on the administrative team as regular members, they will be able to understand better what is going on. They won't have to get information in a second- or third-hand manner. Principals and supervisors ultimately have important functions to perform in the implementation of negotiated agreements. Active representation in the negotiation process facilitates the orientation of administrators and supervisors when it comes time to explain the meaning of the agreement or contract.

Another important aspect of the relationship of principals and supervisors to negotiation is how they are to be represented as categories

[8]Bishop, Leslie J. *Collective Negotiation in Curriculum and Instruction: Questions and Concerns.* Washington, D.C.: Association for Supervision and Curriculum Development, NEA, 1967. pp. 8-9.

of board employees. Are they to be included or excluded from the negotiating unit?

Some assume that the teacher organization which gained the right to negotiate with the administration and the board will decide on the composition of the negotiating unit. If the teachers union is the recognized organization, it is clear that principals and probably supervisors will not be included. NEA-affiliated units may not be so adamant on this point. Nevertheless, the rights of principals and supervisors in negotiation should not be left as a moot issue. Their right to be properly represented must be clear.

The superintendent should have a major part to play in determining the composition of the negotiation unit (unless specified by law). It is possible that the composition of the negotiating unit might be subject to negotiation itself.

If principals and supervisors are excluded from representation in the negotiating unit, they should, nonetheless, have the right to have their interests heard and considered. In larger systems, this may mean separate units for administrators and supervisors. In smaller ones, the rights of principals and supervisors to negotiate with the superintendent and board may be recognized less formally. Each school system should make these determinations in a systematic manner.

*   *   *

It is difficult to specify for each school system the precise roles of administrators and supervisors in negotiation. Monolithic patterns are not feasible. However, each school system should clearly define roles at the outset of negotiation, not leave them clouded or obscure. Since the model of negotiation used has a great influence on role definition, each school system must make its own choices commensurate with its unique requirements.

Preparations

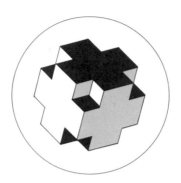

Structure for Negotiation

The subject of negotiation structure was introduced in the section on role definition. There it was indicated that the negotiation procedures developed by a school system depend on many factors and unique local requirements. Among these are size of school system, degree of pressure for formalizing negotiation, state laws on negotiation, attitude of teacher organization(s), attitudes of board members and superintendent, past record on staff relations, and influence of state and national teacher organizations.

Size of school system./Even though it seems obvious that the size of the school system might be the decisive factor in determining the nature and form of organizational structure for negotiation, it is unwise to make this assumption. It is also inadvisable to conclude that all smaller systems follow one pattern and that large systems follow another.

Some smaller systems may have developed elaborate negotiation procedures with some of the characteristics of the larger systems, and the reverse may also be true. On the whole, however, as size increases, negotiation usually becomes more complex and structure more formalized.

Informality is possible when negotiators know each other well—perhaps even on a first-name basis. Previous associations in educational endeavors make highly formalized procedures unnecessary. In fact, to institute them might result in a cumbersome working relationship that could impede rather than facilitate effective negotiation.

In larger systems, where negotiators may meet as virtual strangers, the need for formalized and systematic procedures is more obvious. One of the problems in a large system is the communication gap between top administrators and classroom teachers. This chasm often tends to promote suspicion and cause a lack of faith in the inherent integrity of each negotiating party. It is not uncommon for teachers to assume that superintendents and other administrative officials will put other concerns ahead of teacher wants and wishes. To make more certain that teacher needs are safeguarded, there is an insistence upon carefully drawn rules and regulations to govern negotiation. Thus, formality replaces informality. Negotiation protocol supersedes the unsophisticated give-and-take of informal negotiation.

Degree of pressure for formalizing negotiation./School systems are at different stages in the development of negotiation procedures. Many have already accepted the fact that the process is *fait accompli*. They have adjusted to it, worked out satisfactory procedures, and, perhaps, been through the process more than once. Other systems are at the threshold of formalized negotiation. Still others are in the quiescent stage, having the luxury of a "grace period" during which they can observe, in relative tranquillity, what is going on elsewhere.

Where the process is *fait accompli*, the pressure for formalizing negotiation presumably is past. In the second stage the pressure may be intense, moderate, or slight. Probably no pressure exists at all in the quiescent stage. How does pressure for action affect the structure of negotiation? Where does the pressure originate? Can or should it be resisted?

Pressure to move from informal, *laissez-faire* practices in staff relations with the board and superintendent to structured procedures creates a sense of urgency. It reduces the time for leisurely deliberation and forces those who have the responsibility to act.

These may be pressure just to get on with the task. But, it is also likely that there will be pressure to adopt a particular pattern of negotiation. AFT groups will probably seek a structure that conforms to teacher-union patterns of collective bargaining.

If boards of education and superintendents unduly resist the pressure to comply with the requests (or demands) of the teacher organization(s), tension usually builds up and the possibility of irrational reactions increases. During such periods tempers may become short, thus weakening an orderly movement toward the achievement of a sound negotiation structure. At worst, if things get out of hand, a "field day" of charges and countercharges may result. Accusations and denunciations may be exchanged. News organs of the teacher organizations fan the flames of controversy. This acrimonious atmosphere makes it difficult to develop sound negotiation procedures in an orderly, prudent manner.

On the other hand, there is some good in a reasonable amount of pressure, the type that grows out of a sense of urgency to act. Teachers, administrators, and board members recognize that the times call for change in staff-administrative-board relations. They see the advantage of agreeing upon a new format of interrelationships before forces beyond their control reduce their latitude for action. They wish to avoid the dangers of "too little too late." Self-imposed pressures, mutually applied, are quite different from those imposed unilaterally by one party (usually teachers) upon the others (superintendent and board).

Irrational pressure and irresponsible insistence that the "pot be kept boiling" are disruptive forces and ought to be avoided. Reasonable amounts of pressure are useful and probably necessary in order to hasten desirable changes in staff-administrative relationships.

State laws on negotiation./Almost a third of the states have enacted widely varying statutes related to professional negotiation, and more will come. Some merely authorize negotiation, while others specify, in considerable detail, the shape and substance of the process.

If the state law prescribes the procedures to be followed, local school systems have less opportunity to fashion negotiation structures suited to locally determined objectives. Local options are reduced—or even eliminated.

The pressure for state legislation usually results from local inactivity or even from continued resistance on the part of administration, board, and community to the idea that teachers are eager to formalize negotiation and to achieve a deeper degree of involvement in the making of educational decisions. Thus, it is not an accident that, to date, most of the initiative for introducing negotiation bills in the state legislatures has come from teacher organizations. Administrators and board members, however, through their associations, have come to recognize that they should not sit by and watch bills become laws that mandate a kind of negotiation not particularly well suited to the requirements of the educational system. As more states move to legalize negotiation for school employees, greater attention must be given and more effort made to design statutes that are more applicable to schools.

The significance of state law on the development of the negotiation procedures for local school systems is that much of the structure for negotiation may already be dictated by statute, thus limiting the opportunity for local action. Then, it is primarily just a matter of drawing up a process that conforms to the law. Of course, if the state legislation is a statute of only general authorization, much latitude still exists at the local level to determine the type of the negotiation process to be used.

Widest local latitude for formulating a sound plan for negotiation exists in those states where laws on negotiation do not exist. Teachers, administrators, and board members can take the initiative, without the constraints of law, to write appropriate procedures. It is ironic, though, that the impetus to act is often absent until the prospect of legislation appears on the horizon.

It should not be concluded that the existence of state statutes is presumed to be undesirable. It is only when laws prescribe procedures that require negotiation to take a form that is not well suited to the needs of education that state legislation is considered ill-advised. Well-drawn laws can be quite helpful, and better laws will likely be passed as time goes by. States now contemplating negotiation legislation should study the experiences of others so that mistakes can be avoided and useful practices copied and refined.

Attitude of teacher organization(s)./It is difficult to make specific generalizations about what effect the attitude of the teacher organization(s) has on the development of negotiation procedures for any given school system. It does make a difference whether or not there is more than one organization. If there happens to be more than one, the relative strength of both will have significance, as will the past record of teacher organization influence in the formation of school system policies and procedures. Individual teacher attitudes are also quite important.

There is no way to predict, with certainty, how teachers will react to specific existing conditions or to events that may occur; yet their reactions may have important implications for the development of negotiation procedures.

The best way to ascertain teacher attitudes is to have an ongoing arrangement for teacher consultation in the policy-making and procedure formation, which can be done through advisory councils of various sorts. Teacher consultation is not perfunctory involvement, however; it is deep engrossment in those determinations wherein the concerns and interests of teachers are of prime importance.

A systematic effort should also be made to obtain teacher opinions about the educational problems and issues under consideration. At least, regular "feedback" on the points of view of staff members enables administrators and supervisors to be aware of what staff reaction may be if one course of action is decided over another. This is not meant to imply that administrators must withhold their operational decisions or actions until they "take a poll" of teacher opinion. What is suggested is the wise use of teacher opinion as relevant "data" for making more prudent decisions.

Another dimension of the importance of teacher attitudes and their impact upon the development of negotiation procedures is the rivalry between organizations. The school system, especially the superintendent's office, can get caught in the crossfire if two teacher groups are struggling for ascendency and the right to represent the majority of the staff. On occasion, both the teacher association and the teacher union have used the administration of the school system as the "whipping boy" in their campaigns to win dominance. Where this has happened, it is not surprising that the superintendent and board members have become disillusioned—even bitter—about the viability of the "team approach" and unity of effort in the solution of educational problems.

The large size and complexity of many school systems often create an aloofness between administration and staff. This communication gap may become the *cause célèbre* adopted by competing teacher organizations in promising that they will be more vigorous in fighting for the rights of teachers and will stand up strong and tall against callous administrators if given the right to represent teachers in negotiation. Since "campaign promises" must then be fulfilled after the election is over, this explains why the organization that assumes the most antagonistic posture oftentimes wins in a representation contest. Belligerent attitudes complicate the orderly development of sound negotiation procedures.

Attitudes of board members and superintendent./The attitudes of teachers aren't the only ones that expedite or retard the formation of formalized negotiation procedures. Many board members and superintendents have also resisted the institution of the negotiation process, not from sheer obstinacy, but from an honest conviction that negotiation is not good for education.

Several reasons may account for the apathy or opposition of some board members and superintendents. Many feel that negotiation simply isn't necessary and that the objectives it seeks to achieve can be accomplished just as easily without formalized procedures. Those who hold this view often argue that teachers have the opportunity to confer with the superintendent and to appear before the board of education to state their position on many issues. The argument further continues that since the final determination has to be made by the board of education, there really isn't any point in negotiating because what the board can do is limited by the resources that it has. Another reason for opposition sometimes given by board members and superintendents is that there is no basis in law for negotiation because many states have laws that can be interpreted to mean that boards of education cannot engage in negotiation. Since the law does not explicitly provide for the process, so the argument goes, it is pointless to engage in the process of establishing negotiation procedures that in all probability would have no legal status. ·

It is also argued by some board members and superintendents that the concept of negotiation or collective bargaining is contrary to the professional concept of education itself. It introduces a foreign element in the management of schools. It draws too heavily upon collective bargaining processes used in business and industry. Those who hold this view frequently chide teachers about their alleged professionalism on the one hand and their insistence upon the adoption of procedures of negotiation that seem inimical to the best interests of education.

It is obvious that not all school administrators and board members are opposed to the idea of developing negotiation procedures. The fact that several hundred school systems have adopted negotiation processes indicates that there is a willingness to formalize negotiation. During the last several years, most national conferences of professional associations—particularly those in the area of school administration—have had many sessions on the subject of negotiation. These conferences have influenced the superintendents and board members who have attended them, which may help explain why there has been considerable receptivity toward the idea of having formal procedures in negotiation. These board members and superintendents recognize the inevitability of changes in teacher-administrator-board relationships and have been willing to negotiate

45

effective processes for carrying out these new approaches in interstaff relations.

Past record on staff relations./In those school systems where the administration has been most active in involving the staff in joint decision making, formalized negotiation procedures have often been accomplished with the least difficulty. Moving from voluntary cooperative arrangements to more systematic and well-defined procedures has followed logically. Generally, where cooperation has been practiced most faithfully, the temptation to engage in divisive tactics has been least in evidence.

As pointed out earlier, rivalry between two teacher organizations may change the working relationships of one or both. An organization may have worked most amicably with the administration and the board; but pressure from a rival organization may cause the teacher organization to feel compelled to change and to adopt a rigid and antagonistic attitude toward the administration.

However, where a sound, wholesome, cooperative working relationship has existed for a considerable period of time between the administration and the staff, chances are that the formation of negotiation procedures will proceed with greater ease and with less turmoil. Conversely, where cooperative effort has been at a minimum, an acrimonious atmosphere may cloud the formulation of negotiation procedures.

Influence of state and national teacher organizations./State and national teacher organizations have exerted considerable influence on local teacher associations. At the national level, the strategy of the NEA has focused upon strengthening state associations, enabling them to concentrate in getting state laws passed to improve education in general. State education associations have, in turn, worked to make local associations stronger and more effective.

There has been a tendency for NEA-affiliated teacher associations to shift from operating exclusively in the legislative field and to move more toward applying pressure on the administration and board of education in a local school system for improvements in salary, fringe benefits, and working conditions. In this sense, both national teacher organizations have, especially in the larger school systems, used similar procedures to gain their basic objectives.

Superintendents and boards of education can expect to feel the influence of state and national teacher organizations as they work through local teacher associations and unions. It is not uncommon, especially when recognition elections are in the planning stage, for representatives from the state and national offices of the NEA and AFT to be in the local community and to be prominent in the direction of campaign efforts.

National and state organizations are providing more and more leadership in actual negotiation, especially in crucial situations. Superintendents and board members may regard this as an unwarranted intrusion; yet it is likely to increase rather than go away. It is a condition that has to be met; resentment will not change it.

Preparation for Negotiation

While it is impractical to prescribe a specific organizational structure for negotiation due to the great diversity among school systems and the variations in state laws, it is possible to suggest some general questions that must be answered before the negotiation sessions.

By Administration and Board

1. What negotiation policies or guidelines are to be followed? What will be the rationale for negotiation?

2. What role will be played in the determination of what teacher organization will represent teachers? Will exclusive recognition be granted?

3. Will any effort be made to influence the determination of who will be represented in the negotiating unit? What happens to groups that may be omitted from the unit?

4. Who will do the negotiating? What roles will be assumed by the superintendent, other administrators, and board members? Will "specialists" be used (legal counsel, trained negotiators)?

5. What limitations, if any, will be placed on the scope of negotiation? How will they be decided? Is the scope of negotiation negotiable?

6. What financial and other kinds of data will be needed to begin negotiation? Are these data to be made available to the teacher team?

7. What negotiating strategies should be decided on before the opening session?

By Teachers

1. What posture for negotiation will be assumed? How "hard" will the demands be pushed?

2. Will a certification process or an election be requested to determine who will represent teachers?

3. Who will be included in the negotiating unit, i.e., which groups of employees are to be represented?

4. Who will serve on the negotiating team? How will they be selected? Who will be chief spokesman? Will outside "consultants" be used?

5. What items will be put on the list to be presented? Who determines this? How?

6. How much "research" and fact-gathering will be necessary to support arguments in negotiation? Who collects it? From what sources?

7. What tactics in negotiation are to be followed? Where can help be obtained to sharpen negotiation strategy?

Negotiating sessions./Actual negotiating sessions will vary both in number and in intensity. Some school systems report as many as 300 or 400 clock hours have been needed to reach an agreement. All systems may not require this much time. Certain options are open to administrators and board members in establishing different patterns for negotiation. The following is included merely to illustrate one approach.

47

Illustration of One Pattern of Organization

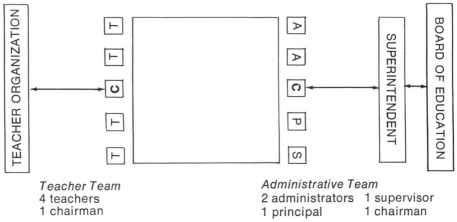

Teacher Team
4 teachers
1 chairman

Administrative Team
2 administrators   1 supervisor
1 principal   1 chairman

This organizational structure places the superintendent as liaison between the negotiating team and the board. This assumes a school system large enough to have enough administrative personnel to whom the negotiation responsibility may be delegated. It further assumes someone among the administrators on the staff who is capable of being chairman of the team. Should conditions not permit the superintendent to remain in a liaison role, he may take direct charge of negotiations as chairman of the administrative team.

Board members are not directly involved in negotiation, remaining instead in the role of ratifiers. This is done (a) to retain the responsibility for direct negotiation in the hands of the superintendent or his designated representative and (b) to avoid placing board members in the position of having to negotiate the details of an agreement that they must later act upon as the legal body charged with the responsibility of granting or not approving the negotiated agreement.

The negotiators designated as administrators might be major department heads having the responsibility for the operation of the major functions of the school system, i.e., instruction, administration, business administration, and so on. Their contributions probably would be as advisers to the chief negotiator, giving advice on the educational implications of various items under negotiation.

It should be clearly understood that the above organization for negotiation is only *one* form. To attempt to describe all the variations that exist would be impossible. The model suggested should not necessarily be considered a recommendation. It is merely an illustration of one approach.

Who Speaks for Teachers

Determining which teacher organization will represent teachers in negotiation is no problem in many school systems, since only one organization exists. But as systems grow larger, more than one organization tends to develop. Usually there is an association affiliated with the NEA and an AFT union. Large city systems, in particular, have these two organizations.

The problem is to ascertain which organization will speak for teachers in negotiation. Two methods are used to determine who speaks for teachers: certification of membership or election.

Certification./The right to represent the teaching staff in negotiation may be established by a certification process. A sworn statement of membership, certification cards signed by individual teachers authorizing one organization to represent them, or other objective evidence of membership in a given organization are the methods most often used. Where only one organization exists, the certification process appears adequate. It only comes into question in those systems having competing teacher organizations.

Unions usually oppose certification processes. They greatly prefer elections, arguing that each teacher should have a free choice, by secret ballot, to show his preferences rather than to rely on membership in a given organization.

Elections./The process of conducting an election to determine the dominant teacher organization for negotiation purposes can be quite involved. Ordinarily, a teacher organization initiates the action for an election. The governmental office controlling negotiation in the state will determine where the petition for an election will be directed. If there is an officially designated body in the state, such as an employment relations board, it will receive the request and conduct the election.

In other situations, a petition for an election may be directed to the board of education which in turn may obtain the services of an organization such as the American Arbitration Association to arrange the details of and conduct the election.

Matters that must be settled in conducting an election are (a) determining which categories of employees are to be included and made eligible to vote in the election, (b) deciding procedural questions concerning the election, and (c) establishing a date for the election.

Reaching agreements on the above issues can entail a great deal of controversy and heated exchange between representatives of teacher organizations. This conflict may be quite disruptive to the school system as a whole.

The administration and board must maintain a neutral position as these decisions are being made. Great care has to be taken not to interfere, hinder, or use influence when representation elections are being planned or are in progress.

A thorny problem arises when two organizations are contesting for the right of representation and are disputing the eligibility of certain groups of teachers for inclusion in the election. If the election is likely to be close, the inclusion or exclusion of a group of certificated personnel such as counselors, psychologists, or other pupil personnel specialists may be a crucial factor.

Another problem may arise on the status of assistant principals, principals, and supervisors in negotiation. Should they be included in the negotiating unit or excluded? Unions usually take the latter position;

NEA-affiliated teacher associations often include them or strive to do so when the conditions of an election are being argued.

Principals may overtly or inadvertently do things that can be interpreted as helping or hindering the teacher organizations in their efforts to win an election. Expediting the distribution of campaign literature of one group and not the other, granting bulletin board privileges to one and refusing it to the other, making favorable comments for one and not the other are examples of actions that usually are construed to be prejudicial. The great danger here is that school officials will be declared guilty of unfair labor practices.

Negotiation introduces many new elements in administrative-staff relations. Previous practices must be re-examined. Administrative neutrality may appear easy enough, yet many cases of alleged partiality have been cited by one organization or the other; and in some of the instances administrators have been judged guilty of violating the neutrality role they are supposed to fulfill. In some states a charge of unfair labor practice would be filed.

Scope of Negotiation

What is negotiable? This is one of the most perplexing questions that arises in negotiation. Some or all of the following items have appeared on negotiation lists.

1. Class size
2. Curriculum
3. Expiration date of negotiation agreement
4. Grievance procedures
5. Inservice education
6. Leave of absence
7. Lunch and rest periods
8. Personnel policy
9. Provision of physical facilities for teachers
10. Recognition of the negotiating team
11. Recruitment of teachers
12. Salaries and wages
13. Teaching assignments
14. Transfers and promotions
15. Welfare benefits.

This list could be expanded to include almost anything in the educational program. Forty-five items appear in the 1967 Agreement signed between the Chicago Board of Education and the Chicago Teachers Union.[1] Thirty items are listed in the 1967 Agreement between the Milwaukee Board of School Directors and the Milwaukee Teachers Education Association.[2]

---

[1]*Agreement Between the Board of Education of the City of Chicago and the Chicago Teachers Union, Local No. 1, American Federation of Teachers, AFL-CIO.* Chicago: the Board and the Union, 1967. pp. 6-63.
[2]*Agreement Between the Milwaukee Board of School Directors and the Milwaukee Teachers Education Association.* Milwaukee, Wis.: the Board and the Association, 1967. pp. 1-26.

The issue of scope in negotiation must be faced squarely. Teachers want it broadened. Pressure will be put on administrators and board members to open all educational matters to negotiation. Teachers are convinced that they are entitled to a more effective voice in determining all those matters that affect their work. They want to be involved in the development of personnel policies and procedures and to re-examine existing policies and procedures. In an effort to expand the scope of negotiation, teachers may insist on being involved in the resolution of problems or issues normally regarded by many administrators and board members as being within the area of administrative prerogative.

Administrative rights./Administrators and board members should think very carefully about the possibility that there may be certain management and board rights and prerogatives that should not be relinquished or made the subject of negotiation. Who is to determine whether certain administrative rights are within the scope of negotiation? Will the superintendent and board of education identify these areas? Or should the areas merely be identified and their inclusion or exclusion be negotiated? However, the scope of the items subject to negotiation may already be specified in those states having statutes governing the conditions of negotiation.

The scope of negotiation will have to be determined in each situation in accordance with all the controlling conditions in a given school system. It is not possible to give exhaustive lists of what should or should not be open to negotiation. However, a decision on this point must be reached before negotiating sessions get under way so that there may be a clear understanding of what can be put on the agenda for negotiation.

Negotiation and advisory consultation./One point of view holds that negotiation should be reserved for only those matters relating directly to salary, fringe benefits, and working conditions. Other items should be designated as topics for staff involvement through advisory consultation in educational decision making, such as the formulation or revision of school personnel policies and procedures, e.g., establishing sabbatical leave requirements.

The difference between negotiation and advisory consultation, as stated in an earlier section, is that negotiation is used to resolve issues about which there may be an "asking and a giving price" at the outset of discussions. Through negotiation, a consensus or as much agreement as possible is reached. Advisory consultation is a process of obtaining and using the opinions of teachers and others in the school system to develop a solution to a problem or to chart a course of action. The item under consideration may be any educational topic. A difference of opinion that has to be reconciled through negotiation may not exist at all.

Teacher involvement in consultation can be just as vital and meaningful as in negotiation. It does not have to be a superficial involvement wherein administrators merely obtain advisory opinion and proceed to act as they please. It is a careful sharing of viewpoints and information, from which a joint decision is reached.

Negotiation might take place only during a concentrated period of time during the school year. On the other hand, consultation may be extended throughout the year in monthly meetings between a teacher committee and the administration. In other words, consultation is more likely to be a year-round activity, while negotiation probably will be limited to a specific period.

Whether this distinction between negotiation and consultation is viable, of course, is a matter of judgment. It does seem, however, that it is a satisfactory rationale for enabling teachers to become partners in educational decision making.

Collecting Negotiation Data

Thorough preparation for negotiation is essential. It is inadvisable to go to the negotiation table without carefully collecting information on the capacity of the school system to grant all or any portion of the requests made by the teachers and other employees. While it may not be practical to "price out" the costs of these requests in advance of their presentation, it is well to know about how far the school system can go toward meeting the requests when their number and nature become known.

Purpose of negotiation data./Effective negotiating cannot be done in a vacuum. A variety of information and data is needed to familiarize negotiators with the past record of the school system in granting improvements in the salary schedule, in the so-called fringe benefit area, and in general working conditions. Good negotiation data provide knowledge concerning the general personnel policies and procedures and the extent to which the staff has been involved in educational decision making. Reliable and current information about salary trends and personnel practices in other school systems is also necessary.

Negotiators on the teacher team may make statements and claims that must be answered or countered. This cannot be done without accurate and up-to-date information. While it may not be possible to have "fingertip" control over every bit of information that may be required, it is possible to have a great deal on the major subject areas.

It is wasteful in time and unwise in strategy to request recesses during negotiation sessions in order to look up certain information or to collect needed data. Ample information, readily accessible, strengthens the hand of a skillful negotiator. Without it, negotiation tends to deteriorate to a level of claims and counterclaims without evidence to substantiate points of view. There is small advantage, if any, in attempting to bluff or to pretend to be informed and knowledgeable without firm data to support assertions or to refute statements made by the members of the "opposition."

Kinds of data./One important type of data is that which describes the financial resources available to pay for the items granted in the agreement. Budget allotments, if any, for salary increases; anticipated revenues from local, state, and national sources during the coming year; the possible need for additional tax levies or allocations from the governmental agency that approves the budget of the board of education; and the estimated costs of various levels of salary increases are the kinds of financial data that are needed.

In addition to available financial resources, various kinds of salary analysis should be made. First, the existing teacher salary schedule, including that for administrative and supervisory personnel, should be available. Secondly, it is well to have a record of any salary or other adjustments that have been made over a five-year period. This will be useful in showing trends in these adjustments. Thirdly, comparative data will be helpful, i.e., existing salary schedules and anticipated increases from school systems of comparable size. These data are useful reference points for comparative purposes.

Fringe benefits are becoming more and more significant in the "monetary package" in negotiated agreements—so much so that the term *fringe* may be a misnomer. Perhaps a more accurate term would be *supplementary* benefits. The logic of viewing these benefits in this manner is that they are an intrinsic part of the total salary adjustment. For this reason, it will be well to evaluate the dollar value of existing benefits, i.e., the value of various kinds of leaves of absence, insurance benefits, hospitalization, vacation allowances (if any), and other negotiated benefits. Salary levels plus supplemental benefits give a more realistic "picture" of what employees are presently receiving.

It is useful, also, to analyze the requests rejected during past negotiation sessions. Rejected items have a way of showing up again on subsequent request lists. The value of reviewing these items is to see if the logic of rejection is still valid or if some merit may perhaps be found for accepting the item if it is re-introduced.

Collecting the data./Collecting, organizing, and assembling the data is an administrative responsibility. Normally, the superintendent will assume this task. In larger school systems, he will likely delegate the responsibility, and in many instances the research office will be given the assignment.

Some school systems have designated an administrator as a director of employee relations. The collection of negotiation data logically could be assigned to his office. This office would correspond to that which business and industry use to handle their employee relations problems. Some of the larger school systems might either designate someone on the staff or employ a full-time specialist to direct employee relations, with his prime responsibility being the conducting of negotiation.

After the initial decision is made on the kinds of data needed, the data must be arranged into a usable format. Voluminous statistics need to be organized in such a manner that the chief negotiator can quickly turn to the salient points supported by the data. A ready summary of the essence of a report, of a survey, or of statistical information is essential. To be obliged to thumb through several pages of data in order to find a bit of information needed to support an argument or to make a point is a handicap and ought to be avoided.

Readily accessible indexed information in a card file or loose-leaf notebook is what is needed. Each negotiator on the team should have a copy of the data, because a team member can often identify the information needed while the chief negotiator continues negotiating dialogue with the members of the teacher team. Teamwork is extremely important in negotiation, and all members of the team not only need the same data but also should be very familiar with it. It should be possible to turn quickly to the exact place needed in the data at any time and come up with facts.

"Homework" needed./Obviously, data must be studied carefully before negotiation sessions begin; and therefore "homework" is necessary so that the negotiators can—

1. Check the accuracy of the information.
2. Avoid the possibility that some necessary data have been excluded.
3. Clarify the implications of the data.
4. Develop a strategy for negotiation which will be supported by the facts which the data reveal.

All members of the team, especially the chief spokesman, must be completely familiar with all the data that have been collected.

Since it is very valuable to have clear, supporting data readily available in order to make a telling point in the heat of negotiation, the possibility of developing charts and visual materials that may be introduced during negotiation needs to be carefully considered.

Sharing of negotiation data./Should the administration share basic negotiation data with the teacher team? There are arguments both for and against this practice. By "sharing data" is meant making basic data available to members of the teacher team. Salary schedules, comparative studies, surveys, and other information constitute the data that can be used to support or refute arguments. Access to the basic data is essential to both parties, and there is little point in denying this access. To do so injects into the negotiation the possibility that the negotiating teams may argue from sharply conflicting "facts." This merely delays progress and increases the possibilities of conflict.

It is not necessary, however, to go beyond the point of making the basic data available. The actual reorganization and interpretation of the information should be the responsibility of each negotiating party.

It should be recognized, however, that the teacher team may not want to rely upon data provided under administrative auspices. It may be felt that data independently collected are preferable. If this is the case, so be it. The point being made is that if teachers want available basic data, they are entitled to them and should be able to get them without difficulty. Both negotiating teams should be arguing from comparable rather than conflicting information.

A "Negotiation Book"

Negotiation data may be organized and put into a "negotiation book," which should be provided each member of the team. The book— a loose-leaf notebook or a card file—should be organized in sections under the major headings or topics included. Numbering items will make it possible to find specific information quickly.

What is included./While each school system will require different specific data, there are certain basic items that will be useful in almost any situation:

1. General policies of board of education with reference to negotiation
2. Policies, if any, that the board follows in making salary adjustments
3. Record of past five years relative to—
   a. Salary increases for teachers
   b. Salary increases for administrators and supervisors
   c. Fringe benefits granted and estimated cost of each
   d. Improvements in general working conditions and cost to the board of education for each improvement
4. Results of survey data from other school systems—
   a. Independently collected data
   b. NEA Research Division data
5. Dollar value of all existing fringe benefits (which may be shown on an hourly, daily, or yearly basis)
6. Number of certificated employees and *average* salary of each category of employee—
   a. Teachers
   b. Auxiliary personnel (counselors, psychologists, visiting teachers, etc.)
   c. Administrators and supervisors (by categories, i.e., assistant principals, principals at each level, central office directors, coordinators, administrators, supervisors, etc.)
7. Approximate amount of money available for salary adjustments and other improvements
8. List of items or requests that the board and administration may wish to present for negotiation with arguments supporting each
9. List of items not granted in previous negotiation sessions, with reasons for rejection (list by years, if possible)
10. To the extent possible, a prognosis of the nature of requests teachers may make in current negotiations with an indication of possible positions to be taken on each.

Once assembled, a "negotiation book" can be kept for use in subsequent sessions; however, as survey and other study data are collected, obsolete information should be replaced with current data. The most efficient way to do this is to assign someone this responsibility on a continuing basis, rather than putting the job off until another negotiation session "rolls around."

The value in having someone on the staff be in charge of negotiation on a continuing basis is that forms and procedures suitable for that particular school system can be developed, kept up-to-date, and refined as required.

Negotiation record forms./Each "book" should have negotiation record forms for the purpose of recording action on each item being negotiated. There are many ways to keep this information, and the form shown in the Appendix is merely an illustration of one way to do the job.

A form to record a summary of decisions made, also illustrated in the Appendix, is suggested as a means of having a complete record of the decisions made on each item. A listing of the items is followed by a brief summary statement of the agreed-upon decision. The form provides a ready reference to what has been decided on every item under negotiation.

Procedures

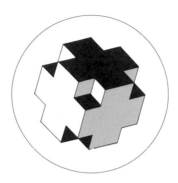

Where and When Sessions Are Held

Ordinarily there should be little or no difficulty in determining where and when to hold negotiating sessions. Complications can develop, however. Clear understandings should be reached on the following matters.

Place of meetings./Negotiation meetings may be held either on or off board of education property. Suitable facilities may be available in the central office headquarters or a school building. Sometimes the teacher team may be reluctant to meet on school property, preferring instead to meet on "neutral grounds," such as a convenient motel or hotel.

The place of meeting is a joint decision of the negotiating parties. Presumably, the chairmen of the two teams can confer and make this decision.

Type of facilities./Three rooms are essential—one large enough for the negotiating sessions and two adjoining it, one for each negotiating team. Adjacent rooms facilitate recesses for team conferences by saving "travel" time to and from the main negotiating room. Good physical accommodations—proper lighting, heat, ventilation, table, chairs, water, glasses, soft drinks, coffee, rest rooms—are also essential.

Time of meetings./This is another matter to be agreed upon by the negotiating parties. It would seem that sessions ought either be held during the day, perhaps from nine to four-thirty or five, or in the afternoon and early evening, perhaps from one to five. In the first instance the sessions will take place entirely on school time, and substitute teachers will have to be provided for an entire day for those teachers on the teacher team. Depending upon the number of sessions, this could mean that children might be deprived of their regular teachers for a considerable period of time.

In the second instance, teachers might meet with their classes half a day; a substitute would continue for the other half. Also, this means that negotiation sessions would be about 50 percent on school time and 50 percent on the time of the teachers.

It is not wise to hold sessions exclusively in the late afternoon and far into the night. It is too much to expect negotiators to put in a full day's work and then to negotiate after the work day when fatigue may become a limiting factor. Bad decisions can be made when the negotiators are physically tired.

Scheduling of meetings./Presumably, certain negotiation sessions will be concentrated in a given period of time. The time of year varies from system to system. If salary adjustments are effective at the beginning of a school year, i.e., in September, concentrated negotiation sessions will probably take place in the spring. If salary adjustments are made on January 1, the sessions will usually be held in the fall.

It is wise to start early enough to give time to get the job done well. Trying to pack too many sessions into a limited period imposes pressures that complicate negotiation.

In the case of advisory consultation, i.e., those meetings where the topics under consideration involve longer range issues, such as the development of a personnel policy or modification of an existing policy, monthly sessions may be scheduled for the greater part of a year.

In business and industry, it is usually necessary to give 60 days notice of a desire to open negotiations. In those states having negotiation laws, the amount of advance notice that must be given before the initial session begins may be stipulated, so that local negotiators do not have to make the decision. Where such is not the case, it is wise to give ample time to get ready for negotiation, certainly from 30–60 days notice.

The details necessary for conducting subsequent negotiation sessions may be agreed upon at the initial session or at the end of each session for the next meeting.

It is well that key officials of the teacher organization, the administration, and the board be aware of the schedule of negotiating sessions and hold themselves available in case members of the negotiating teams should need their counsel or advice. Other details regarding negotiation sessions should be agreed upon as local conditions require.

Before the Second Meeting

During the interval between the initial and second meetings, several things need to be done. The most important task is that of making a careful analysis of the requests made by the teachers. This will involve estimating the monetary costs of the requests, analyzing their educational implications, and determining the most appropriate strategy to follow in subsequent negotiating sessions.

Estimating the costs of requests./This is extremely important. It is essential that estimated costs be checked against the available resources of the school system. If these costs markedly exceed available revenues, this fact must be taken into account. It should be recognized, however, that the decision to grant salary and related requests doesn't always depend upon available revenues. Sometimes salary policies dictate adjustments for which funds may not be on hand. In this case, it must be understood that additional funds will have to be obtained in order to meet committed policy.

It may be difficult to ascertain the costs of every request on the list. Some items do not lend themselves readily to cost analysis. Yet, not to make an effort to arrive at a general estimate is to put the school system at a disadvantage in negotiation. A total "price tag" is needed in order to proceed intelligently.

The educational implications of requests./Many requests have important educational implications, the significance of which must be carefully assessed. Some may affect or alter existing instructional policies and procedures. Some requests may, if granted, affect the manner in which principals operate their schools. Some, also, may seek to modify existing personnel policies and procedures.

In the analysis of requests, those so-called "middle managers" (principals, directors, and supervisors) who are in the best position operationally to advise as to the wisdom of granting or rejecting a request should be asked to do so. They can be very helpful in providing arguments for and against the request. There is another important reason for involving these intermediate administrators and supervisors. As has earlier been indicated, they need to feel involved in negotiation and their expertise will be very useful in the formulation of a tenable position which will stand up in negotiation.

Primary and secondary issues./In every list of requests some items will be regarded as being more significant than others. It is usually expected that more items will be included than will be granted. This is part of the give-and-take of negotiation.

It is well to speculate on which items are prized more highly than others by the teacher team. In other words, are there some items which the teachers regard as indispensable to an acceptable agreement? If so, which ones are they?

This sorting of primary and secondary requests is useful in that it helps the administrative-board team members become sensitive to the "must items" on the list, not that these requests must always be granted.

But, at least, it may help in negotiation dialogue to avoid head-on collisions on sensitive issues.

Determining negotiation strategies./There are no prescriptions which will guarantee that negotiation will go as either team prefers it. The team chairman—and each member of the team for that matter—will do well to school himself in some of the techniques of effective negotiating. The suggestions that follow are similar to those made in a recent negotiation conference conducted by the Ohio School Boards Association.

1. *Keep calm—don't lose control of yourself.* Negotiation sessions can be exasperating. The temptation may come to get angry and fight back when intemperate accusations are made or when "the straw that broke the camel's back" is hurled on the table.
2. *Avoid "off the record" comments.* Actually nothing is "off the record." Innocently made remarks have a way of coming back to haunt their author. Be careful to say only what you are willing to have quoted.
3. *Don't be overcandid.* Inexperienced negotiators may, with the best of intentions, desire to "lay the cards on the table face up." This may be done in the mistaken notion that everybody fully understands the other and utter frankness is desired. Complete candor doesn't always serve the best interests of productive negotiation. This is not a plea for duplicity; rather, it is a recommendation for prudent and discriminating utterances.
4. *Be long on listening.* Usually a good listener makes a good negotiator. It is wise to let your "adversaries" do the talking—at least in the beginning.
5. *Don't be afraid of a "little heat."* Discussions sometimes generate quite a bit of "heat." Don't be afraid of it. It never hurts to let the "opposition" sound off even when you may be tempted to hit back.
6. *Watch the voice level.* A wise practice is to keep the pitch of the voice down even though the temptation may be strong to let it rise under the excitement of emotional stress.
7. *Keep flexible.* One of the skills of good negotiators is the ability to shift position a bit if a positive gain can thus be accomplished. An obstinate adherence to one position or point of view, regardless of the ultimate consequences of that rigidity, may be more of a deterrent than an advantage.
8. *Refrain from a flat "no."* Especially in the earlier stages of negotiation it is best to avoid giving a flat "no" answer to a proposition. It doesn't help to work yourself into a box by being totally negative "too early in the game."
9. *Give to get.* Negotiation is the art of giving and getting. Concede a point to gain a concession. This is the name of the game.
10. *Work on the easier items first.* Settle those things first about which there is the least controversy. Leave the tougher items until later in order to avoid an early deadlock.
11. *Respect your adversary.* Respect those who are seated on the opposite side of the table. Assume that their motives are as sincere as your own, at least until proven otherwise.
12. *Be patient.* If necessary, be willing to sit out tiresome tirades. Time has a way of being on the side of the patient negotiator.

13. *Avoid waving "red flags."* There are some statements that irritate teachers and merely heighten their antipathies. Find out what these are and avoid their use. Needless waving of "red flags" only infuriates.

14. *Let the other side "win some victories."* Each team has to win some victories. A "shut out" may be a hollow gain in negotiation.

15. *Negotiation is a "way of life."* Obvious resentment of the fact that negotiation is here to stay weakens the effectiveness of the negotiator. The better part of wisdom is to adjust to it and to become better prepared to use it as a tool of interstaff relations.

To some extent these guidelines oversimplify an intricate process that requires knowledge, insight, and patience. Time and experience are necessary in the development of expertise in the art of negotiation. Both—prudently employed—will increase negotiating effectiveness.

Subsequent Sessions

Since the first session merely introduces the requests made by the teacher group, actual negotiation begins with subsequent sessions. At the second session, the administrative team chairman reacts to the teacher requests. Prior administrative caucuses presumably will have resulted in tentative positions on the items on the request list.

The agenda./The proposals made by the teacher team and those made as counterproposals by the administrative team become the items on the agenda. Once both sides reach agreement on which items will be on the agenda, it should be agreed that no new ones will be added.

General reaction./The chairman of the administrative team may make a brief statement, reporting that the "package" appears excessive in its total demands. Issue may be taken with some of the rationalizations behind certain requests. A willingness to look favorably upon some of the items may be expressed, but the members of the teacher team are to understand that a hard look is going to be given each item.

Response to general reaction./The teacher team chairman may reiterate his conviction that his team's requests are realistic—even conservative—and that teachers are not going to retreat from their determination to get a substantial salary adjustment, related benefits, and a larger share of involvement in day-to-day decision making.

After these skirmishes have ended, serious negotiation begins. An agreement may be worked out to establish a priority order for discussing the various items. It is not unusual to put less controversial items at the top of the order of discussion, leaving the more difficult ones for later consideration.

Analysis of items./One approach is for the administrative team to give a brief response to each request. Each item may be deemed acceptable, unacceptable, deferrable, or modifiable. As a matter of strategy, unqualified acceptance is usually given with great reluctance, at least in the earlier sessions. Likewise, outright rejection is usually avoided.

In other words, extreme positions are shunned if at all possible. The more likely attitude will be one of qualified acceptance or rejection.

Sometimes a counterproposal will be introduced suggesting a different approach, a proposal to lessen the amount or content of an item, or an entirely different proposition may be offered. This may be done with recognition that the counterproposal stands little or no chance of being accepted by the teacher team. It is done with the hope, nevertheless, that pressure and persistence for the original request may be lightened somewhat and a less demanding attitude may be assumed insofar as that item is concerned.

The administrative team may ask that a given item be deferred for the time being. This is not rejection; it is merely an attempt to get the item off the list for the time being with the understanding that it may be reintroduced at another time.

As items are discussed and agreements reached, they should be properly recorded on the form provided, and each team chairman should initial the agreed-upon terms.

Team unity./Team members should learn how to work as a well-coordinated unit. Depending upon the area of specialization of each member, the chairman may want individual members to speak to certain requests. In all instances, however, the chief strategist should be the team chairman. There can be only one captain.

If possible, each session should yield one or more agreements on specific items. This gives a sense of achievement and reduces the frustration level. Early deadlocks should be avoided if at all possible. They tend to get negotiation "off the track" and prolong discussions.

Negotiation and advisory consultation./It has been pointed out earlier that items on request lists may be of two kinds: (a) those related to salary, supplemental benefits, and working conditions, which if granted will involve a substantial outlay of money, and (b) "noneconomic" items, which are more closely identified with personnel policies and procedures or some phase of the educational program.

The former usually must be resolved through negotiation because of the divergence between what is requested and what is offered. The latter, having longer range implications, conceivably may be decided through consultation rather than negotiation. If these items can be so identified and if agreement can be reached that they may be handled in this manner, negotiation sessions may be reduced in number. At least, an effort should be made to distinguish negotiation from consultation items and an attempt made to deal with them accordingly.

Number of sessions./There is no way to predict the number of negotiation sessions needed to reach a final settlement. Experience has shown that a range of from a few meetings to as many as 35 or 40 (in some cases, even more) may be required to reach final agreement. When this amount of time is consumed, it is apparent that negotiation has become a major administrative activity for all who may be involved. This is why an increasing number of school systems are considering the advisability of establishing a separate office to conduct negotiation on a continuing basis.

The Road to Agreement

It is not surprising that some hazards mark the road to agreement. Difference of opinion is inherent in negotiation. The parties start with divergent points of view and work toward consensus. Disagreements are likely to arise. Some deadlocks may even develop. It is, therefore, essential to be aware of and sensitive to some of the possibilities of breakdown in negotiation before a final agreement is attained.

It is possible that, ultimately, an impasse may occur, but only after extended, good-faith negotiating has failed to narrow the gap of widely divergent points of view. Lesser divergencies, i.e., pitfalls on the road to agreement, may also result in an ultimate impasse; and efforts should be made to avoid as many of them as possible. Among the danger signs are the following:

Bending the facts Danger lurks in arguing from sharply conflicting facts and information. Reliance should be placed upon data that honestly and accurately describe the financial condition of the school system. Salary studies should be completely and fairly reported. All other information used by the negotiating parties to substantiate their positions should be valid and reliable. There may be legitimate differences in the interpretation of basic data; this is understandable. On the other hand, if either or both parties deliberately try to "bend the facts" to suit their purposes or to gain an advantage, the possibilities of consensus are greatly lessened.

Toying with the truth Deliberate and persistent overstatements and exaggerations to gain an advantage reduce confidence in and respect for the integrity of the party that indulges in these excesses. Recklessness in negotiation serves no useful purpose and jeopardizes the chances of agreement.

"Molehills and moun-tains" A temptation may arise to overemphasize an issue or to defend a point of view far in excess of its real importance. In fact, a negotiator may pursue a point with such emotional fervor that it is presumed to be of supreme importance to him. Actually, however, the effort may be a "smoke screen" or a diversionary tactic to mislead the opposition. In the long run, a procedure of this kind creates confusion and generates disagreements.

Ignoring need for victories Negotiation, by its very nature, is a contest between proponents and opponents of a point of view relative to a particular issue being negotiated. Conceivably, one side could be so formidable that it could overpower the other and force the weaker team to capitulate on all points at issue. This may only be a Pyrrhic victory, for each side needs to have some success. Wise negotiators recognize the soundness of this fact.

Discounting the "oppo-sition" Underestimating the acumen and competence of one's opponent in negotiation is unwise. Inexperience may result in some degree of ineptitude in debate. But, as in the story of the tortoise and the hare, it is never prudent to underestimate an opponent. To do so not only is disrespectful but also engenders the risk of eventual discord.

Premature Maintaining reasonable flexibility in negotiation is advisable.
inflexibility Some may argue that flexibility is synonymous with weakness, that "firm negotiation" involves taking a defensible position and refraining from retreat. In other words, stand firm once a position has been taken. To defend this concept of "hard negotiation" is to risk the accusation of failure to negotiate in "good faith." Early hardening of positions increases the danger of premature deadlocks.

*　*　*　*

These are some of the danger signs of troubled negotiation. To ignore them is to invite undue conflict. Part of the problem is inexperience. Once past this period, negotiators begin to see the wisdom of honest "give-and-take." To compensate for inexperience each team should have as many experienced negotiators as possible. In lieu of experience, training sessions will be useful. In fact, many teacher organizations conduct training workshops and clinics. Manuals and handbooks stressing negotiation "knowhow" are being developed. Some administrators may deplore these efforts but in the long run they should be welcomed as a means of achieving a level of maturity and sophistication that will increase negotiation effectiveness. Administrators probably will find it advantageous to engage in similar inservice training.

Mediation, Fact Finding, and Arbitration

Deadlocks may occur from time to time. It is presumed that every effort has been made, through good-faith negotiation, to reach an agreement and that all such efforts have failed. When this situation prevails, the disputing parties feel obliged to turn to some ultimate measures to achieve a settlement. Mediation, fact finding, and arbitration are three of these terminal procedures.

These methods are common in labor-management collective bargaining but not so prevalent in educational negotiation. However, since impasse procedures may utilize variations of these techniques, it seems useful to describe the essential elements of each.

Mediation./This is an action that continues the negotiation process but with the assistance of a third party who may be invited in to assist in achieving a settlement.

Either or both parties may request mediation. The request may be initiated more frequently by the teacher team. Although only one party initiates the action, the other usually acquiesces, even if the desire to do so may be less than enthusiastic.

The mediator seeks to understand the issues that divide the parties and strives to reconcile opposing points of view. He proposes alternatives and promotes compromises. Separate and joint sessions are held in an effort to achieve consensus. Mediation is a voluntary process, and recommendations are purely advisory and nonbinding.

Fact finding./Fact finding, which normally follows mediation, is a process by which the facts and issues in a dispute are carefully examined, written findings are prepared, and recommendations are made to settle the dispute. When fact finding becomes necessary, it is usually a clear indication that everything else has failed and negotiation is in danger of complete breakdown.

An individual, a panel, or a board may do the fact finding after a reasonable period of good-faith negotiation results in a stalemate or when one or the other negotiating party persistently refuses to engage in good-faith negotiation. While the fact finder's recommendations generally are not binding on either negotiating party, there is an inclination for both to accept the recommendations because of the publicity that they usually have received by this time. Public pressure ordinarily is sufficiently strong to cause the negotiators to feel that it would be inadvisable to ignore the recommendations.

Arbitration./As a final recourse, negotiation deadlock may be resolved by means of arbitration. This is a process wherein a third party is called upon to render a decision that is generally final and binding, unless legal restrictions prevent a board of education from agreeing to binding arbitration.

If both parties agree in advance to submit a dispute to arbitration and further agree to accept the recommendations of the arbitrator, the arbitration is said to be *voluntary*. If the law requires arbitration in order to prevent a cessation of work or a stoppage of services, it is regarded as *compulsory*. It is considered a last-resort technique.

Some hold that it is unrealistic to suggest arbitration as a means of settling an impasse on the grounds that a board of education cannot or should not agree to a procedure that binds its hands in passing on the ultimate decision. This point of view rightly points out that a public body, such as a board of education, should not agree to assume a financial obligation—which might be imposed by an arbitrator—that exceeds its resources. Even a fiscally independent board might hesitate to assume a financial commitment that would require the voters to approve a sizable extra tax levy in order to pay for the cost of the agreement awarded by the arbitrator. A fiscally dependent board would be in an even more vulnerable position to agree to binding arbitration.

Admittedly, these procedures may sound strange to many school administrators, except in those states in which negotiation follows labor-management patterns. It is useful, however, to be familiar with these techniques because as time passes they may become more common even in so-called "nonunion" negotiation. Certainly in larger cities these procedures may very well become a part of the negotiation process.

The natural sequence in negotiation moves from less formal give-and-take to more formalized negotiation procedures, especially if roadblocks are encountered. The diagram below illustrates the progression in negotiation procedures.

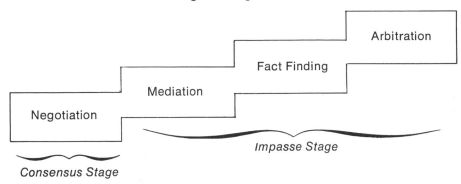

Grievance Procedures

One of the products of negotiation usually is the development of grievance procedures. These provide a systematic way to resolve aggravated complaints by means of sequential steps moving progressively upward through the administrative structure of the school system.

It should not be assumed, however, that there were no formalized grievance procedures before the advent of negotiation. Many school systems with well-organized personnel departments have worked out good procedures as a part of a sound personnel program. In those instances, however, where the procedures had not been formalized, it has been customary to make their development one of the primary objectives of negotiation.

Complaints and grievances./There is a difference between a complaint and a grievance. The former may be regarded as a problem or difficulty arising frequently at the local school or office level and involving a difference of opinion between two persons. Not infrequently the parties are a teacher and an administrator. In the normal course of events, the issue can be resolved at the level of origin by the parties concerned, in which case the matter does not result in a grievance.

A grievance is an intensified complaint that cannot be resolved informally by the parties involved; and, consequently, the complainant feels obliged to seek redress by referring it to the next highest level in the organization of the school system.

Grievance procedures, therefore, are designed to solve intensified complaints rather than day-to-day problems, disputes, or differences of opinion originating at the operational levels of the school system. The significance of this distinction is that when a request is made to apply the grievance procedures, the nature of the complaint must be considered to make sure it is a true grievance.

Inclusion in negotiated agreement./Leslie G. Young of the Alberta, Canada, School Trustees Association points out that there are two components in effective grievance procedures. One is stated in the negotiated agreement and the other in the personnel rules and regulations of the school system. According to Young, the component listed in the agreement should contain—

1. The definition of a grievance.
2. The formal procedure for the resolution of grievances, which should specify—
   a. The maximum allowable time for processing at each step.
   b. What happens if time limits are not observed.
   c. The stage at which the grievance must be articulated in writing (remember, over 90 percent are settled at the oral presentation stage), in short, the who, what, and when at each step.
3. The authority of the arbitrator usually restricted to applying the agreement or to interpreting it (keep in mind that the arbitrator is the employee of the disputant parties).
4. Procedure for appointment of arbitrator(s).
5. How costs of arbitration are to be met.
6. Who may bring a grievance—bargaining unit, teacher, board—and who may appear on behalf of the grievor.[1]

Implementation./The proper implementation of the procedures is the key to their success. Ordinarily, the personnel rules and regulations of the school system contain the detailed steps of the grievance procedures. Young has also provided the following suggestions to guide in the formation of operational grievance procedures:

1. Allow for the easy lodging of complaints.
2. Provide for prompt but complete, careful, and considered investigation of all complaints.
3. Immediate sifting of complaints from grievances.
4. Impartial treatment and protection from reprisal for those lodging complaints. This should not be necessary but it is to be remembered that grievances usually originate as redress for alleged abuses of administrative initiative.
5. Provide for resolution of grievances at the lowest possible level of the administrative hierarchy, thus strengthening line of authority.
6. Assure informal handling of complaints during primary presentation.
7. Treat all grievances confidentially.
8. Support junior administrators when dealing with employees, but reprove them privately as necessary. It is essential to prevent administrative leap-frogging.
9. Improve operating efficiency.[2]

Common procedures./All classifications of employees should have access to grievance procedures for the settlement of their aggravated complaints. It would be well if the same procedures, instead of several different ones, could be used by all employees. Some school systems have succeeded in doing this by forming a joint committee, representing both certificated and classified employees, to work with the administration in

---

[1]Young, Leslie G. "Grievances-Impasse." *Teacher-Administrator-School Board Relationships.* Minneapolis, Minn.: Educational Research and Development Council of the Twin Cities Metropolitan Area, 1967. p. 109.

[2]*Ibid.,* pp. 109-10.

developing common procedures. Where it is not possible to do this, one set for certificated personnel and another for classified or noncertificated employees are developed.

Most employee problems can be settled without resorting to the use of the latter stages of the formal grievance procedures. Since the initial stage is oral dialogue between the parties involved, an overwhelming number of complaints never advance beyond this stage. It has been estimated that only about 10 percent of employee complaints go beyond the initial talking stage.

Purpose of procedures./The advantage of written grievance procedures is primarily to give employees the assurance that their complaints may be resolved in an orderly manner and without reprisal. At the same time, administrators can be more sure that their rights may be properly protected. Sometimes allegations may be made by teachers against administrators, charging arbitrary and unwarranted use of executive power. Grievance procedures provide a sound way to test the validity of these allegations. They offer administrators assurance that if their behavior is reasonable and fair, their actions may be vindicated.

Grievance procedures should be designed to fit the requirements of each school system. Variations will appear in procedures even for systems of comparable size. Organizational structure, philosophy of administration, and employee attitudes will govern the form and substance of the procedures.

Considerable help in drafting grievance procedures is now available in the literature. Lieberman and Moskow provide useful suggestions and give examples of three types of agreements.[3] It may also be useful to collect copies of procedures used in other school systems and study their successful techniques.

Formalizing and Ratifying the Agreement (Contract)

After negotiation has been completed and a consensus has been reached, it is essential that the agreement (contract) be put in written form to prevent misunderstandings or any temptation to disaffirm the agreement in part or as a whole.

In an earlier section it was suggested that a running record be kept of the action taken on each item on the list and that each team chairman initial agreements reached. This continuing record simplifies the preparation of the final agreement.

Preparation of written agreement./The responsibility for formalizing the final agreement rests with the members of the negotiating teams, and the process of preparing the document may differ from place to place. A subcommittee, representing both teams, may be designated to draw up the final agreement. When completed, the total membership of both teams is convened to read and approve the text of the agreement. Or, the chairmen of the teams may prepare the final draft for approval by the entire membership of the teams.

---

[3]Lieberman, Myron, and Moskow, Michael H. *Collective Negotiations for Teachers: An Approach to School Administration.* Chicago: Rand McNally, 1966. pp. 350, 608, and 651.

In some instances the task of preparing the final draft may be assigned to one who specializes in drafting agreements. This could be a lawyer or it might be a representative of the research department of the school system. This person must have attended all negotiating sessions and must be fully familiar with all the details and records of the negotiating sessions.

In yet other situations the entire membership of the negotiating teams might prepare the final draft after agreement has been reached. This approach is probably the least effective of all those mentioned.

Language of the agreement./It is essential that the agreement be worded in a manner that leaves no "loopholes" and avoids ambiguities. The text should clearly reflect that which was agreed to, and care should be exercised to avoid embellishments that tend to include more than that actually agreed to.

It must be remembered that the final agreement not only has to be ratified by the board of education and the teacher organizations designated to represent the staff, but also has to be implemented by administrators, supervisors, and teachers once it is signed and becomes effective. Thus, to go overboard in using legalistic language may confuse more than clarify an understanding of the document by those who must put it into operation.

Tentative and final drafts./It may take quite some time to put the agreement in a final form acceptable to both parties. As changes are made, it is important that members of the negotiating teams are made aware of the modifications and give their approval. When at last the final draft has been completed and approved, it is ready to be submitted to the ratifying agents, i.e., the board of education and the teacher organization.

Ratification./It is understood that both negotiating teams will recommend acceptance of the final agreement to the parties whom they represented in negotiation. Should it become necessary, for any reason, for either or both of the ratifying parties to request a change or an amendment in the agreement, it is recognized that the modification should properly be referred to the negotiating teams for pro-and-con discussion of the modification. Generally, the ratifying parties will make only minor changes, which can be incorporated readily without reopening full-scale negotiation.

Release of information./Both negotiating parties should work out a satisfactory understanding of how the contents of the agreement will be released to the staff and to the public. Care must be taken to prevent "leaks" and other premature release of information. The ground rules for making the contents of the agreement known should be discussed and agreed upon by the negotiating parties well in advance of the presentation of the document for signing by the ratifying parties.

Every effort should be made to let nothing happen at the last minute to mar the efforts of the negotiators, who have worked diligently to bring about a satisfactory agreement. Improper release of information may cause difficulty.

Putting the Agreement into Operation

It may be assumed that the major job is done once an agreement has been satisfactorily negotiated and ratified. However, while it is true that the importance of this time-consuming task should not be underestimated, the actual implementation of the agreement is of equal, if not greater, significance.

Much of the good work of the negotiators may be undone if, for some reason, those responsible for the operations of the school system fail to carry out the requirements of the agreement. For this reason it is essential that the contents of the agreements be thoroughly communicated to all administrators and supervisors at the local school and other levels in the organization.

Role of local school administrators./Principals and assistant principals have important roles in the implementation of agreements. An examination of some completed agreements reveals that many items relate to the administration of a local school. The following subjects, found in several agreements, illustrate areas of direct concern to local school administrators: relief from nonteaching chores, extra duty assignments, limitations on number of teaching periods per day, programs for teachers of special subjects, duty-free lunch periods, limitations on class size, teacher transfers and rotations, use of teacher aides and assistants, and limitations governing the daily teaching program.

Local school administrators must be familiar with the provisions of the agreement that alter policies and procedures governing the administration and supervision of their schools. This familiarization process may be accomplished in different ways.

Principals may be represented on the administrative negotiating team either actively or as observers. These representatives will thus be informed about items of direct significance to principals and assistant principals, as well as the pro-and-con discussion on these topics. At the close of negotiation they will be able to report to their colleagues on the implications of the agreement for local school administrators.

If not represented in direct negotiation sessions, principals and assistant principals must be thoroughly briefed by the superintendent or his designated representative after the agreement has been signed and is ready for implementation. This involves placing a copy of the full agreement in the hands of each principal and assistant principal with complete explanations and comments to promote a full understanding of the relevant items in it.

If local school administrators, whether inadvertently or consciously, disregard or violate the requirements of the agreement, it can be expected that grievances will be filed.

Central office administrators and supervisors./While central office administrators and supervisors may not have direct operational responsibility for administering the agreement, their actions may create conditions that may impinge upon the implementation of the agreement.

It is equally important, therefore, that top administration include all administrators and supervisors, regardless of level, in briefing sessions.

They too should have copies of the agreement and be urged to read it carefully, especially those sections directly related to their areas of operational responsibility.

Teacher orientation./It is equally important that teachers be familiar with the contents of the agreement. It is presumed that the teacher organization will assume major responsibility for this orientation and for distributing copies of the agreement to the teachers. There is no reason, if the negotiating parties have discussed and agreed upon a plan, to exclude the administration of the school system from this orientation. Ways and means for communicating the contents of the agreement to the entire staff must be found, regardless of how it is done or who does it.

Monthly meetings./Many agreements stipulate that monthly meetings be held between teacher representatives and the administration to discuss problems and issues which may arise in the implementation of the agreement. These meetings may be a part of the ongoing advisory consultation program in which teachers share in decision making (referred to earlier), or they may be separate meetings expressly designed for reporting and resolving infractions in the implementation of the agreement.

Feedback./It seems reasonable to assume that the implementation of an agreement is a "two-way street." Grievance procedures provide ample opportunity for teachers to get redress for their complaints. It is probable that they will be alert to any administrative actions that may be interpreted as violating the teacher rights provided for under the terms of negotiated agreements.

It is equally important for operational level administrators and supervisors to ascertain if the terms of the agreement are being observed by teachers and to be alert to any weaknesses in the agreement from the standpoint of the operation of the school system.

The Road Ahead

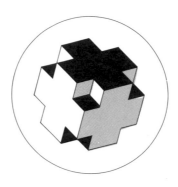

The impact of negotiation has been felt in various ways by different school administrators. Some have been catapulted into a maelstrom of negotiation without much warning and with minimal preparation. Others have moved into it in a more deliberate and orderly fashion. Still others have not had to engage in formalized negotiation at all. It is no wonder that administrators' opinions of the process vary so widely.

Though the trend toward the passage of more state laws on negotiation is definite, there are still several states in which school systems have gone more or less untouched by these "winds of change." Relatively minor modifications have been required in administrative-staff relations.

What lies ahead? Some say that the future will be marked by a rapid spread of negotiation. Teacher militancy will intensify. The need for greater administrative expertise in negotiation will increase. There are some who say that more cleavages between classroom teachers and administrators will develop and with greater rapidity.

Less pessimistic "prophets" believe that professional unity can be maintained in teacher-administrative ranks. In fact, proponents of the principle of harmony in the profession believe that it is not necessary for administrators to go down one path and teachers another. Division merely weakens the structure of education and introduces elements of discord that undermine the administrator's role as an educational leader.

Realism dictates, however, that administrators recognize that a strong possibility exists that the decision for or against continued unity in the profession may be dictated by the teachers themselves. Administrators may have less to say about the matter than they think. Only time will tell.

It may be useful here to examine some of the possibilities that lie ahead, not for the purpose of making predictions but to sharpen insights and to anticipate future developments more accurately.

1. Will differences between teachers and administrators become more pronounced?/Possibly. The potential for divergence probably is greatest in the city and in large, suburban school systems because of (a) the heightened rivalry between the two major teacher organizations and (b) the size of the school system itself, which tends to weaken communication between chief administrators and teachers. The complexity of the problems to be solved is also a contributing factor. It is easier to make administrators, especially the superintendent, a target for complaints and to attribute to him the responsibility for most of the frustrations that many teachers feel. Hostility toward the superintendent and his administrative staff may be overt in some instances. At other times, it is subtle but, nevertheless, present.

Not all teachers, however, feel this antipathy toward administrators. The impetus for its existence and spread most frequently comes from the more militant members of the staff. They tend to believe that the interests of teachers are better served by divorcing teaching from administration. They prefer a posture of teacher *vs.* administrator rather than teacher *and* administrator.

It is inaccurate to conclude, however, that the cleavage between teachers and administrators pervades the total profession. The close, harmonious working relationships that exist in many school systems will continue.

The meaning of this conflicting condition is that each superintendent has to assess the teacher-administrator climate in his own system and decide whether a pattern of negotiation can be built upon unity of purpose and a framework of cooperation or whether a dichotomy of purposes and objectives prevails. This assessment is necessary in determining both the structure and the process of negotiation.

2. Will the format of negotiation in education become more and more like that used by labor and management?/While this is a distinct possibility, much will depend upon the architects of negotiation—teachers and administrators.

In some systems considerable pressure may be exerted by teachers to duplicate the collective bargaining model; while in others, this tendency will not be great. Since school systems vary so widely, it is unwise to generalize on what will happen.

School administrators themselves have an obligation to press for a form and format of negotiation that will best serve the needs of education. They are in a position to exert strong influence in achieving this goal. To let the direction which negotiation may take go by default is to neglect an important leadership responsibility.

There is no reason not to "borrow" useful aspects of labor-management collective bargaining techniques, however. Since education is a relative newcomer to the art of negotiation, it should be able to profit from the lengthy experience that business, industry, and labor have had with the process.

The point being made is to fashion negotiation in a manner that makes it serve education as effectively as possible, recognizing the unique requirements of school systems and the purposes for which they are organized.

3. Is negotiation in education obliged to duplicate all the growing pains that labor-management collective bargaining has experienced?/It is significant that in recent years, there have been examples where both labor and management have been able to work together with sufficient harmony to prevent long-drawn-out, acrimonious negotiating sessions. Many of the stresses and tensions that have characterized collective bargaining in the last quarter of a century can be bypassed if teachers and administrators use good judgment in working out their negotiating relationships. The nature of the educational enterprise justifies this hope.

If salary policies are negotiated with the staff, it is conceivable that the implementation of those policies can be achieved without extensive negotiation sessions. This is not meant to imply that ways should be found to avoid negotiation, rather that negotiation need not be an extended period of tension-laden, hard-nosed bargaining. The process should be a responsible exchange of viewpoints, the presentation of proposals and counterproposals, and a sincere and determined effort to reach a consensus fulfilling the reasonable expectations of both parties but not at the expense of the educational enterprise itself.

It is fully recognized that this goal is idealistic. Maturity in negotiation is not achieved through exhortation. There will undoubtedly be some necessity for a clash of opinions and a need for a degree of forensic "combat." Each party is obligated, however, to make negotiation as professional a process as possible and to avoid deliberate actions calculated to make it only an exercise for selfish fulfillment.

4. Does negotiation institutionalize conflict?/It may do so, but it doesn't have to. If negotiation is perceived and designed as a process for legitimatizing the orderly exchange of teacher-administrator viewpoints on issues of concern to each, this type of give-and-take interchange does not have to be considered as institutionalized conflict. The participants may make it so, but if this occurs it is more the fault of the participators than the process.

Negotiation may result, in its initial stages, in the sharing of certain leadership prerogatives with teachers. This can be construed as a surrendering of administrative power and a lessening of the administrator's authority. Some administrators regard it so. Some even resist going to the negotiation table. When this occurs, teachers may press all the harder for recognition of their "right" to negotiate. This can result in conflict.

On the other hand, many school systems have moved into negotiation without acrimonious clashes. Teachers and administrators have recognized that an orderly and systematic exchange of points of view on an expanding number of topics can be productive and in the best interests of the school system.

The ways and means of negotiation will differ widely. In the search for a sound process for teacher-administrator interchange it should be kept in mind that negotiation can be a constructive force in staff relationships provided the parties involved perform in a spirit of goodwill and respect. This must be a two-way street, however; and good-faith negotiation presumes honesty and integrity on the part of all concerned. Given these basic ingredients it can and should be a valuable instrument for improving teacher-administrator relations.

Appendix

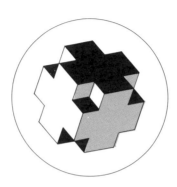

Compendium./Several terms have been used in this analysis of negotiation. This compendium is included for ready reference and indicates the definition or position taken with regard to each term.

Term or Item	*Definition/Position Taken*
Administrator's role in negotiation	School administrators (below the rank of superintendent) will have different roles in different school systems. Their principal functions will be to provide information, review and react to items on the negotiation list, advise the superintendent, and assist in the implementation of the negotiated agreement. In some instances, their representatives serve on the administrative team.
Agenda	The finally agreed-upon list of requests (demands) and counterrequests that become the items for negotiation. Generally, once the agenda is agreed upon, no new items are added to the list.

Agreement (contract)	The finally agreed-upon document, which contains the terms of the negotiated contract and which binds the parties to certain actions for a specified period of time.
Accountability in negotiation	A principle that holds that each negotiating party should be held answerable for its actions by some higher authority, e.g., board of education is responsible to the public; the superintendent to the board of education.
Analysis of requests	The process by which items on the negotiation list may be examined to ascertain their economic costs and educational implications.
Arbitration of impasse in negotiation	A procedure of final recourse designed to resolve a negotiation deadlock (impasse) wherein a third party is called in to render a decision usually accepted by the negotiating parties as final and binding.
Arbitration of impasse in grievance procedure	An impasse may occur in the resolution of a grievance, i.e., no mutually satisfactory solution may be reached, even at the terminal step in the process. In such an instance, the parties may agree to submit the grievance to an outside arbitrator whose decision may become binding.
Attitudes toward negotiation	The viewpoints and/or biases of teachers, administrators, and board members, which can produce a climate of either acceptance or disapproval and which either facilitates or obstructs negotiation.
Board of education in negotiation	Bears the ultimate responsibility for representing, in negotiation, the school system as an institution and the public interest. This responsibility is fulfilled by delegating the negotiation responsibility to the superintendent of schools and by holding itself as the ratifying body.
Collective bargaining	The process by which teachers, through their designated representatives, negotiate with the board of education, through its designated representative(s), with reference to salary, working conditions, and other matters of interest to the negotiating parties. Collective bargaining usually follows a labor-management format.
Complaint	A problem that may or may not develop into a grievance. It normally occurs at an operational level either in a local school or office. It often involves a teacher or other employee and an administrator or supervisor and may be resolved without becoming a grievance.
Conciliation	A term often used in the same sense as mediation. It involves the service of a third party whose purpose is to help the negotiating parties reach a voluntary agreement without any form of coercion.

Consultants	Those called in by the negotiating parties to provide expert advice and opinion about some aspect of the subject(s) under negotiation.
Fact finding	A process of investigation of an impasse in negotiation for the purpose of ascertaining the relevant facts and analyzing the issues that underlie the dispute, so that a report may be filed with recommendations for a settlement.
Good-faith negotiation	Negotiation that is conducted honestly and forthrightly and that avoids any attempt to subvert the process or to put obstacles in the path toward a satisfactory agreement.
Grievance	An aggravated or intensified complaint that cannot be settled at the operational level and has to be resolved through the grievance procedure.
Grievance procedures	The sequential steps through which aggravated complaints may go in being satisfactorily resolved, the progression being upward through the hierarchical ranks of the organization.
Impasse	A deadlock reached after a reasonable period of good-faith negotiation and which the parties are unable to resolve without "outside" assistance.
Legal counsel	An attorney with expertise in negotiation who gives advice in the carrying out of the process. He may or may not engage in direct negotiation. One or both parties may have legal counsel.
Mediation	A fact-finding and advisory process of interpreting, counseling, and suggesting to the negotiating parties possible ways to solve an impasse in negotiation, such recommendations not being binding.
Negotiation	Systematic process whereby teachers (or employees) and the board of education (through designated representative) may negotiate matters of mutual concern with provisions for the resolution of possible impasses in negotiation. While the process of negotiation may resemble collective bargaining in form and technique, it is usually structured to conform to the educational setting.
Negotiation "book"	A systematically assembled account of items on the negotiation list analyzed for cost and educational implications, plus provisions for a running account of the action taken on each item.
Negotiation climate	A state of mind or attitude of the principal negotiating parties ranging somewhere on a continuum from mutual receptivity and acceptance to general hostility.
Negotiation data	The facts and figures assembled—in advance of actual negotiation—to assess the economic and other resources of the school system and an analy-

sis of the estimated costs of the items on the negotiation list as presented for consideration.

Negotiation laws — Statutes passed by state legislatures governing the conduct of negotiation in a given jurisdiction and establishing the general guidelines under which professional negotiation in individual school systems may be carried out.

Negotiation and advisory consultation — Processes by which teachers and other school employees exert a voice in determining the decisions, conditions, and policies under which the school system operates. *Negotiation* assumes a divergence of initial positions reconciled through the give-and-take of good-faith negotiation. *Advisory consultation* consists of cooperative staff involvement through consultation to solve problems or to reach mutually satisfactory decisions on issues of concern to the parties involved.

Negotiating parties — Individual(s) representing the teachers (or other employees) and the board of education (or its designated representative) who meet to consider items on the negotiation list and who seek to achieve an agreement satisfactory to both parties.

Negotiation record — Consecutive account of action taken on each negotiated item showing the position of each party and the conclusion reached in each instance.

Negotiation sessions — Formal meetings of the negotiating parties at which pro-and-con arguments are presented with reference to the items under negotiation.

Negotiation strategy — Tactics employed by each party in arguing its case in its effort to attain the objectives for which it is negotiating.

Negotiation teams — Individuals engaged in actual negotiation—one group representing teachers or other employees, the other representing the board of education. Size and composition of the two teams varies by school systems.

Negotiation unit — Categories of employees that will be represented by the organization designated by the teachers (or other employees) and recognized as such by the board and administration.

Recognition agreement — Formal acknowledgment by the board of education of an employee organization—officially designated—to represent teachers and/or other employees in professional negotiation.

Record of voting — Systematic consecutive account of decisions reached on each item on the negotiation list.

79

Representation by certification	Procedure wherein recognition is granted to an employee organization to serve as the negotiating agent with the board of education (through designated representative) on the basis of certified membership records, signed authorization cards, or other techniques which will indicate the majority organization without recourse to a formal representation election.
Representation by election	Process of determining the organization that will serve as the negotiating agent with the board of education (through designated representative) by means of a secret ballot.
Sanctions	"Censure, suspension or expulsion of a member, severance of relationship with an affiliated association or other agency; imposing of a deterrent against a board of education or other agency controlling the welfare of the schools; bringing into play forces that will enable the community to help the board or agency to realize its responsibilities; or the application of one or more steps in the withholding of services . . ." [1]
Scope of negotiation	Limitations (if any) placed upon the kind and number of items or issues that may be presented for negotiation by either or both parties.
Strike	An action of last resort taken by employees when an extended impasse in negotiation occurs and that results in work stoppage or cessation of service.
Summary of decisions	Summary of actions taken on all items on the negotiation list, thus providing a written record of decisions reached.
Superintendent's role in negotiation	Depending upon the requirements in different school systems, the superintendent may perform a variety of functions ranging from "bystander" with no direct responsibility for negotiation to chief negotiating spokesman representing the board of education.
Teacher wants	The aspirations and expectations of teachers that may become the underlying motivations for the formation of specific requests for negotiation.
Union affiliation	Identification with a labor-oriented organization (union) rather than a teacher association for the purpose of engaging in negotiation.

[1] National Education Association, National Commission on Professional Rights and Responsibilities. *Guidelines for Professional Sanctions.* Revised edition. Washington, D.C.: the Commission, 1966. p. 9.

Specimen Copy

Action Report

Item	Accept as stated		Accept as revised		Reject	
	1	2	1	2	1	2
1. Increase of $1,000 at maximum and $500 at minimum of teachers' salary schedule *(Revised statement)*						
2. Board pays 100 percent of Blue Cross and Blue Shield *(Revised statement)*						
3. Two additional paid holidays *(Revised statement)*						
4. Seniority must be given first priority in granting all transfers *(Revised statement)*						
5. Maximum of 30 pupils in elementary and no more than 28 in secondary classes *(Revised statement)*						

Etc.

1. *Chairman of teacher team initials*
2. *Chairman of administrative team initials*

Item	Decision agreed to:	Initials	
		1	2
1. Increase of $1,000 at maximum and $500 at minimum of teachers' salary schedule	*$750 at maximum; $350 at the minimum*		
2. Board pays 100 percent of Blue Cross and Blue Shield	*50 percent of total cost first year; 75 percent of total cost thereafter*		
3. Two additional paid holidays	*Accepted as stated*		
4. Seniority must be given first priority in granting all transfers	*Seniority may be dominant factor in 40 percent of transfers*		
5. Maximum of 30 pupils in elementary and no more than 28 in secondary classes	*Deferred for further consideration*		

Etc.

1. *Chairman of teacher team initials*
2. *Chairman of administrative team initials*

Bibliography

Allen, Roy B., and Schmid, John, editors. *Collective Negotiations and Educational Administration.* Columbus, Ohio: University Council for Educational Administration, 1966.

American Assembly. *Challenges to Collective Bargaining.* Englewood Cliffs, N.J.: Prentice-Hall, 1967.

American Association of School Administrators. *School Administrators View Professional Negotiation.* Washington, D.C.: the Association, 1966.

Bishop, Leslie J. *Collective Negotiation in Curriculum and Instruction: Questions and Concerns.* Washington, D.C.: Association for Supervision and Curriculum Development, NEA, 1967.

Chamberlain, Neil W., and Kuhn, James W. *Collective Bargaining.* Second edition. New York: McGraw-Hill Book Co., 1965.

Doherty, Robert E., and Oberer, Walter E. *Teachers, School Boards, and Collective Bargaining: A Changing of the Guard.* Ithaca: New York State School of Industrial and Labor Relations, Cornell University, 1967.

Douglas, Ann. *Industrial Peacemaking.* New York: Columbia University Press, 1962.

Epstein, Benjamin. *Principal's Role in Collective Negotiations Between Teachers and School Boards.* Washington, D.C.: National Association of Secondary School Prinpals, NEA, 1965.

Henderson, James A., and others. *Creative Collective Bargaining.* Englewood Cliffs, N.J.: Prentice-Hall, 1965.

Illinois University, Institute of Labor and Industrial Relations. *Collective Bargaining for Professional and Technical Employees.* Urbana: the University, 1965.

Law, Kenneth L., and others. *The Manual for Teacher Negotiators.* Windsor, Conn.: Educational Consultative Services, 1966. 56 pp.

Lieberman, Myron, and Moskow, Michael H. *Collective Negotiations for Teachers: An Approach to School Administration.* Chicago: Rand McNally, 1966.

Lutz, Frank W., and Azzarelli, Joseph J. *Struggle for Power in Education.* New York: Center for Applied Research in Education, 1966.

Mabry, B. D. *Labor Relations and Collective Bargaining.* New York: Ronald Press Co., 1966.

Metzler, John H., and Knade, Oscar, Jr. "A Tranquilizer for Negotiations." *American School Board Journal* 155: 12-13; December 1967.

Moskow, Michael H. *Teachers and Unions.* Philadelphia: Wharton School of Finance and Commerce, University of Pennsylvania, 1966.

National Education Association, Division of Urban Services. *Professional Negotiation: Key to Better Teaching Conditions.* Washington, D.C.: the Association, 1966.

National Education Association, Division of Field Operations and Urban Services. *Introduction to Professional Negotiations.* Washington, D.C.: the Association, 1966.

National Education Association, Office of Professional Development and Welfare. *Guidelines for Professional Negotiation.* Revised edition. Washington, D.C.: the Association, 1965.

National Education Association, Research Division. *Negotiation Research Digest* 1: B-1 to B-7; September 1967.

National Education Association, Research Division. *Professional Negotiation with School Boards.* Research Report 1965-R3. Washington, D.C.: the Association, March 1965. 44 pp.

Personnel Management Service, Division of Educational Service Bureau. *The Techniques of Negotiation in Public Education.* Arlington, Va.: the Bureau, 1966.

Randle, Clinton W. *Collective Bargaining.* Second edition. Boston: Houghton Mifflin, 1966.

Schmidt, Charles T., Jr.; Parker, Hyman; and Repas, Bob. *A Guide to Collective Negotiations in Education.* East Lansing: Social Science Research Bureau, Michigan State University, 1967.

Stinnett, T. M.; Kleinmann, Jack H.; and Ware, Martha L. *Professional Negotiation in Public Education.* New York: Macmillan Co., 1966.

Walton, Richard E., and McKersie, Robert B., editors. *A Behavioral Theory of Labor Negotiations: An Analysis of a Social Interaction System.* New York: McGraw-Hill Book Co., 1965.

Warner, Kenneth O., editor. *Developments in Public Employee Relations: Legislative, Judicial, Administrative.* Chicago: Public Personnel Association, 1965.

Wynn, D. Richard. *Policies of Educational Negotiation—Problems and Issues.* Pittsburgh: Tri-State Area School Study Council, University of Pittsburgh, 1967.

Young, Leslie G. "Grievances-Impasse." *Teacher-Administrator-School Board Relationships.* Minneapolis, Minn.: Educational Research and Development Council of the Twin Cities Metropolitan Area, 1967.

PB-5923-858-BRACK.PAM
75-39T